No contacts? No problem!

How to pitch and sell a freelance feature

methuen | drama

Methuen Drama

1 3 5 7 9 10 8 6 4 2

First published in Great Britain in 2009 by Methuen Drama

Methuen Drama
A & C Black Publishers Ltd
36 Soho Square
London W1D 3QY
www.methuendrama.com

Copyright © Catherine Quinn, 2009

Catherine Quinn has asserted her rights under the Copyright, Designs
and Patents Act, 1988, to be identified as the author of this work

A CIP catalogue record for this book is available
from the British Library

ISBN 978 1 408 12356 0

Typeset by Margaret Brain, Wisbech
Printed and bound in Great Britain by Martins the Printers

No contacts? No problem!

How to pitch and sell a freelance feature

Catherine Quinn

Contents

Acknowledgements   vii

Introduction   ix
    Who this book is for   ix
    The 'No Contacts' philosophy   xii
    How to use this book   xiv

1   **The pitch – at the heart of freelancing success**   **1**
    What is a pitch?   1
    Writing a good pitch   4

2   **Knowing the market – what's out there?**   **8**
    Maximising your chances of success   9
    The freelance marketplace   14

3   **Red-hot leads – narrowing your focus**   **23**
    Drawing up your dynamite list of leads   23
    Narrowing your focus   27
    Contacting the editors   31

4   **Not so fast! Before you pitch**   **38**
    The three elements of a winning pitch   39
    Stretching to fit – making your pitch fit the market   40
    Mistakes to avoid   45
    Professionalism – it's a state of mind   47

5   **Ready ... set ... pitch!**   **51**
    The ideas factory – what makes a saleable feature?   51
    Compelling writing   55
    Structuring your pitch   58
    Sending out your pitches   66

6   **Help! I don't have any clips**   **70**
    Clips – the Catch 22 of the first-timer   70
    Getting around the issue of clips   75
    How to get real clips   79
    Celebrity short-cuts   81
    Using the web to showcase your work   85
    Beyond writing – pitching in person   85

7	Chase-ups – the most important part of your job	91
	They haven't got in touch – they hate my ideas!	91
	The importance of chase-ups	94
	How to chase	94
	Rejection – your golden opportunity to appear professional	98
	Keeping track of what you pitch	101
8	Your first commission	107
	Maintaining the professional front	107
	Different types of brief	110
	Asking the right questions	111
	Other issues	114
	Copyright	116
	Pictures	119
	Expenses	120
	The 'can-do' attitude – yes to everything	121
9	Writing the thing	123
	Don't panic – it's not too difficult to write articles	123
	How long should I take?	125
	Establishing the tone of your feature	126
	What should go into it?	127
	Interviewing	131
	Getting good pictures	132
10	Keeping 'em coming	136
	Don't give up your day job	136
	The sordid topic of coin – how much should I be paid?	139
	Rewrites	141
11	Tricks of the trade	147
	Tricks to get good sources	147
	PRs – your dynamite resource	150
	Writers' perks	154
12	And finally ...	160
	Marketing is all	160
	The entrepreneurial curve	161
13	The four-week plan	164
	Useful information and further reading	170

Acknowledgements

Special thanks to my publisher Jenny Ridout for taking a chance on a new book in tough economic times (and throwing a free lunch into the deal); to Susannah Quinn for providing valuable insights; and to Kevin Harris for being my best friend and keeping a secret.

Thanks so much to everyone else who helped me through this project, directly or otherwise. To Andrew Stock, Jim Tann, Paul Ferris, Alex Button and Phil Holland at 72 Cromwell Road for being my unwitting support act. Not to mention Laura Langthorne, Lucy Yates and Becca Rose.

Then of course there's the lovely Victoria Ward, Andrew Williams and Andrew Shanahan for being the joint funniest editors; Barbara Rowlands and Jan Goodey for being good enough to share their tutors' expertise and quick enough to divulge tips on the spot; Emily Dubberley for taking the time, as always, to respond to a request for help at lightning speed; Jeroen Bergman for sharing his pet peeves; and Susie Tempest for telling us why PRs are not so bad after all.

Finally a big thanks to all of you readers and new writers who are coming into this industry to make it a fast-paced and exciting environment for us all.

To my sister Squeezy, who is a better
writer than I'll ever be

Introduction

Who this book is for

If you want to get something published in a national newspaper or magazine but you have no idea how the process works, then this book is for you. Like many people looking to 'break into' journalism, you may be wondering whether it's possible to start out as a freelance feature writer, and if so, how you can get that vital first piece in print.

If you've found that the process is mysterious and that those in the know are somewhat unwilling to spill the beans on how it all works, you're certainly not alone. Freelancing is a notoriously guarded subject area, not least because many who make a living from the process have done so by building up contacts over a number of years.

The good news is there *is* a way in at ground level, even with no experience and no contacts. Given that you have the talent and motivation, anyone can get their work published in a national newspaper or magazine – without connections, experience, or a family member on the editorial team.

The information in these pages will be invaluable to you if you are:

- A student on a journalism course, or a student on any other course looking to get into print or journalism.
- A career changer, or job seeker hoping to crack the business.
- A current freelancer keen to expand your net and approach editors not formerly known to you.

You will also find this book very useful if you are:

- Committed to attaining a staff role on a publication, and know that examples of your work in print will help you achieve this.
- Thinking of going into PR, press relations or marketing, and

looking to enhance your knowledge of how to get your clients in the press.

- Have a 'big idea' for which you're keen to get national exposure.
- Want to use published newspaper or magazine features as a springboard into another area of writing.

The 'No Contacts' method outlines a tried and tested way for writers with no published work to get that vital first commission in a national publication. It lifts the lid on the systems which even established staff writers take years to learn, and outlines a fast-track technique to getting your work commissioned by top publications.

Just the facts
If you've already read a few books aimed at freelance writers, you'll notice that plenty of them tell you how to write well, and a few offer useful tips for established freelancers. But when it comes to a book which explains how to go from no clips at all to a published piece in a national newspaper, suddenly the publishing world draws a blank.

Because this book outlines the nuts and bolts of freelance feature writing for the absolute beginner, it focuses primarily on the process of pitching ideas, rather than writing features. You won't read about the grammatical nuances of a great feature in these pages (although you will learn what makes a great *idea* for a feature). Neither will you discover how to maximise your income levels, specialise, serialise or syndicate your work. That all comes later, because if you're starting out, your primary concern is *how to get published in the first place*.

What you will learn about in detail is what goes into a pitch that gets commissioned, how to focus and target the magazines which offer you the best chance of getting in print, and how to follow through and chase up your pitches to get them published.

No Contacts? No Problem! will show you how to:

- Work with the processes used by editors to commission new writers.
- Identify what makes a winning feature idea.

- Understand the formats which make editors buy ideas.
- Learn how rejection can be turned to your advantage.
- Deal with having no clips to show editors.

Once you've got a commission using this book, the rest is up to you. If you're dedicated, then practising the techniques outlined in these pages should be all you need to springboard your first few features into a long-term writing career. And once you've got started, there are a number of resources available which can help you further hone your ability to get work, make money and write great features. Some of the most useful are listed in the recommended reading section on pages 170–72.

You can write – right?
The 'No Contacts' method does assume a few things, though. This is a fast-track technique for writers who know they've got what it takes. So firstly, it's assumed that you can write well enough to be published in a national publication. If that sounds daunting, tough: you're either ready to start freelancing or you're not. If you don't have the confidence that you can produce this standard of writing, then take a writing course, buy a book on grammar, or do whatever you need to do to get your writing to the necessary standard before attempting to use the method outlined here.

If you feel that your writing is good enough to be paid for by a newspaper or magazine, then you're ready to get started. It's not assumed that you will have the experience of an established freelancer when it comes to how quickly you can turn out quality work, or that you know anything much about freelancing. Just that you have the potential to get faster at attaining that professional quality and will put in the effort to learn your trade.

How much do you want to be in print?
Do you really *really* want to be in print? If the answer to that question is anything other than a firm 'yes', then this book isn't for you. The strategy outlined is only effective when combined with dogged determination and a lot of hard work. If you want to take an easier, longer route, start looking for a staff job. The 'No Contacts' route is like an intensive training course – you'll get there faster, but it's much more effort in the short term.

If you're only half sure, or thinking of dabbling, then – to put it bluntly – forget it, at least as a career. Freelance feature writing is incredibly competitive and there's very little room for people who think they 'might' want to do it. You could get lucky, and use the techniques in this book to hit on a commission immediately. But it's more likely that you'll have to endure at least some rejection when you're moving towards your first published article – and a lot of knock-backs if you're putting the procedures in place to become freelance full-time. You'll get there in the end, but someone who's anything less than 100% dedicated will most likely find the rejection hurdle too difficult to overcome.

Here's the good news, though. If you know your writing is of a high enough standard to be published, and you're prepared to work hard to get something in print, then the processes outlined in this book are your ticket to that first commission.

If this seems like a bold claim, it's not. Although reading this book and putting the system into practice is straightforward, it will also involve plenty of dedication and effort from you. There are no practice questions here – everything you're shown how to do is the real thing, tailored for editors of current publications.

Once you've got your action plan underway, you'll be committing fully to conducting your own intensive training course. At the end of it you'll have learned first hand, through your own experiences, what makes it into print and what doesn't. Not to mention having built up a comprehensive knowledge of which magazines are easiest to get work from, which editors get back to you quickly, and which you should write off. This book may provide you with the course content, but it's you who'll be putting in all the hours.

So, are you ready to get your work published using the 'No Contacts' method? Then let's get started.

The 'No Contacts' philosophy

If you've invested your time and money in a well-known journalism course, or slogged it out as a staffer for years, you will have earned one thing for your troubles, and that's confidence. When you're starting out from scratch with no editors to recommend you, and no portfolio of published work to prove your abilities, confidence is harder won. But it's key to getting published the 'No Contacts' way.

If you're ready to put this method into effect, then your watch-words from now on are **confidence, determination** and **professionalism**. Each is a vital component of your future success, and you can't get published without all three.

Confidence

The techniques in this book rely on your unwavering faith that you have the ability to get into print. You need to have that already – or at least the capability to learn it and put it into practice. The reason why this book offers a fast-track to top writing assignments is that it relies on your ability to rapidly learn to adopt the professional traits which will convince editors to commission your work.

The good news is that you'll build confidence using the 'No Contacts' method, as your systematic pitching and chase-ups bring you positive feedback. It may also comfort you to know that many freelancers who have been in the business for years are still a little under-confident that they can really make this pitching thing work.

So a core part of what you'll learn in this book is how to become confident in your abilities, and how to appear confident to the editors you approach. How you present yourself and the esteem in which you hold your work are integral to the philosophy of making this book work for you.

Professionalism

Another reason why this technique is so successful is that it places an emphasis on professional conduct. What you'll learn above all else is to approach your freelancing like a business, using established industry know-how and sales strategies. Rather than contacting editors with the attitude that they're doing you a favour by listening to your proposals, you're going to understand why you have a valuable commodity to offer them.

Just like any other business, your focus will not be on the emotional goal of 'being a writer' but on the practical achievement of getting your start-up business into sales and profits. When you learn to see the editor as a customer, you'll distance yourself from the tendency to imagine them as a kindly soul who will look favourably on your efforts and give you a hand-up into the industry. Instead, you will understand that only saleable material will get you in print, and your work will shift accordingly.

Professional behaviour will be a motif which you'll work on throughout your training period. Once you've put that behaviour at the heart of how you send out work and speak with editors, the rest will follow.

Determination

It goes without saying that you'll need to be determined, but dedication comes in many forms. You won't be learning how to beg for work, hound editors, or generally place yourself at the bottom of the dogsbody pile. But you will learn how to efficiently and professionally chase up your work, utilise tools to help you stay focused and motivated, and understand how to avoid excessive rejection.

How to use this book

This book is set out like a training programme, with core learning outcomes stated at the beginning of each chapter, and exercises for you to complete at the end. If you're committed to the process, it's important that you read the book from start to finish, following the exercises and without skipping valuable information.

You should dedicate around a day of your time to completing each set of exercises, and, as most involve contacting real-life publications, you need to allocate this time to a nine-to-five week-day, with access to email and a telephone.

The text explains everything you need to know to work the publication process and get your features considered by top editors. It also includes REMEMBER points – vital gems which many freelancers wished they knew when they started out, and sections called 'Learning the hard way' – freelancing lessons learnt by trial and error which you can get right first time. There are also plenty of editors' tips ('A word from the editors') to give you an overview of professional opinion.

Web tips

Everything you need to know is contained in these pages, but there is also a comprehensive online resource available to accompany the book at <u>www.nocontactsnoproblem.com</u>. Here you can post questions on a dynamic forum and access a number of very useful resources, including pitch examples, links to trade magazine sites, recommendations of journalist request sites and editors' tips.

The site also contains advice on building databases for those ready to take their career to the next level, and provides an option to download a highly effective ready-made database, custom-built for start-up freelance journalists.

1

The pitch – at the heart of freelancing success

This chapter is about setting the scene for how successful freelancers operate and how they engage editors to commission them. You'll learn about what pitching is, the fundamentals of how the process works and, most importantly, why you don't necessarily need any contacts to get involved.

In this chapter you'll:

- Learn what to send to editors to gain a commission.
- Understand the best formats for getting your ideas considered.
- Know the industry-standard methods of approaching editors for work.
- Begin to analyse why certain articles make it into print.

If you've read this far, you're probably hungry to know what you should be doing to get into print. So I'm going to cut to the chase and give you a taster on the fundamentals of freelancing. This chapter outlines the heart of what freelance writers do to get into print – or to put it another way, it covers *pitching* – the core activity of a successful freelancer.

What is a pitch?

If you're unfamiliar with the print industry, the process of going from unknown writer to someone who is regularly published in national publications may well be a total mystery. Some people assume that work experience is the way to put themselves in an editor's sights; others send off examples of their writing, or features aimed at a publication's style; and a fortunate few will make a couple of calls to friends or family members and land themselves a paid position on a publication.

In fact, none of these techniques is particularly effective when it comes to getting full features published within a reasonable time-scale. The good news is that there is a much quicker way to be commissioned as a professional freelance writer – and better yet, it's based on merit.

A freelance writer will pitch *ideas* to an editor in the hope of securing a commission for a full piece, and this is where the great leveller of raw talent comes in. It doesn't matter if you've worked as a builder all your life, or if you're fresh out of school; if you're capable of sending in good ideas, you're capable of gaining commissions from national publications.

This is the case even if you are fortunate enough to have those all-important 'contacts' in the newspaper and magazine world. Editors can't run bad ideas, even if the person sending them is a family friend or close relative. But a person who regularly sends them great ideas will quickly attract their attention in a commissioning capacity.

REMEMBER: **Editors don't buy writing. They buy ideas.**

So ... do you just send in articles, then?

If I had a commission for every time I've been asked this question, I'd need a couple of staff members by now.

The short answer is 'no', I never, ever send in full articles without them having been commissioned – and neither should any freelancer, experienced or otherwise. It's one of those infuriating myths that writing is so dependent on the *artiste* that the Cinderella new-writer will dash off a heartfelt opinion piece, and an editor prince or fairy godmother will fall in love with their style and instantly give them a column.

If I were working as an interior designer, I wouldn't approach a potential client with a room I'd already decorated to his or her taste. Nor as an accountant would I calculate a potential client's annual tax return to show how well I could do it. The process of writing is a business like any other, and a writer's time is no less valuable than any other professional's. With this in mind, a writer, much like an interior designer or an accountant, should never hand out their skilled services for free as a tool to beg for further work. Instead, we discuss a client's needs prior to negotiating the terms of employment – not least to assure ourselves that the task in hand would result in payment.

What should I be sending in?

All very well, you may think, but how do you go about getting the commission in the first place?

Now we've established that editors are looking for great ideas, the next step is to find out how to deliver them in a format they want to commission. In order to do this, freelancers send a 'pitch' (or several) to a likely editor. When you send a pitch, that's exactly what you're doing: pitching for work. The pitch is a sales document, if you like, of your potential to write about a particular topic which by its nature is short and to the point. You're enticing the editor to want to buy the whole article.

More importantly, sending in a short 'pitch' rather than a full-length article is a badge of your professionalism. If you're very keen to get into print and know you're a good writer with great ideas, it might be tempting to send an entire article to show an editor just what you're capable of. But just to reiterate, this is something a professional freelancer would *never* do, and it will immediately alert an editor to the fact that you probably don't write for a living.

Why is pitching the best way in?

Magazines and newspapers don't just randomly fill pages with copy that is loosely based on their predominant themes. Most have rigid plans into which articles of specific lengths and topics must fit. This can be based on advertising, or simply an editorial whim to keep certain slots addressing certain topics.

A speculative idea or article might be absolutely timely and perfect for the magazine, but because of logistical issues like advertising may not be right for an up-coming edition. So your article on juniper jam might be vetoed for a piece on strawberry jam, simply because a strawberry jam manufacturer has bought up a number of adverts in the magazine.

If you've sent a short pitch and it's been rejected, then it's no problem. But if you've put together an entire article, you've not only wasted your valuable time on work which won't be paid for, but you've also marked yourself out as a newcomer to an editor, who will not be expecting, for the most part, to receive fully written articles from freelancers. (The only exception to this, incidentally, would be if you were a writer offering syndicated work that had already been published elsewhere, in which case you would be expecting a lower fee and marketing the piece as a reprint.)

Hopefully I've now managed to completely put you off sending in finished features to sell your ideas. From now on, when you're writing you're working, and as a freelancer your work is valuable. Which means you send a synopsis first, and write up an article only when you're guaranteed payment. Remember you *are* a professional. Even if you're not yet in print.

Writing a good pitch

In order to get published, then, you must adjust your focus from those well-written features you read in magazines, and shift it towards a writing format you'll never see in print – the pitch format.

REMEMBER: **At the heart of a successful freelancing career is not the finished article, or even the great idea, but the successful pitch.**

A good pitch is essentially a well-written synopsis which will convince an editor to buy you as a writer. It is a showcase – not only of your writing abilities, but more importantly, of your ability to identify an idea which will grab a reader's attention.

In essence the pitch is a bite-sized piece of writing which neatly delivers a great idea, encompassing the angle that the writer suggests should be covered, and what will be included in the finished article. But the winning pitch will state a great idea in a way which compels the reader to want to know more.

A word from the editors

"People will tell you a lot about how freelancing is a very difficult job and that you'll struggle to earn a living, but it certainly needn't be if you always follow this one simple piece of advice: have better ideas than everybody else.

That's it. Simply originate and execute ideas that are better than the ones that everybody else has. If you're in an editorial meeting and pitching stories – have better ideas than everyone else has. If you're writing an article and it seems like the most mundane subject on earth – have better ideas about how it could be covered than everyone else has. If you've not worked for six weeks and you're wondering where you can find an assignment – have better ideas about where to generate work than everyone else has."

Andrew Shanahan, freelance writer and columnist, *The Guardian*

There are many ways to put a pitch together, and you might end up with a favourite that is different from what is outlined here. However, for beginners I would recommend a format known as the classic 'head-sell' as the best way to sell an idea. This format is well structured for a newspaper or magazine, because rather than selling the concept of what a story might include, it goes straight in to how the story will be written.

The head-sell basically starts with an opening paragraph about how the article will begin, followed by four or five bullet points as to what the body text would cover. By now I imagine you'll want to see what this kind of pitch looks like. The following is one which secured me several commissions from national newspapers, including *The Guardian* and *The Times*. You'll notice that I've included a headline and a 'standfirst' (the introductory line of text below the headline), as well as an opening paragraph and bullet points of how I expect the article might progress.

Web tip:
If you're starting out, you're probably anxious to see as many tips as possible. Luckily you can access an archive of tips at www.nocontactsnoproblem.com/pitchexamples.html

[HEAD]

Written Evidence

[STANDFIRST]

Be careful who you write to, warns Catherine Quinn. It could be revealing more than you realise.

[BODY]

There was once a time when neat, legible handwriting was a prized skill in office work. But in our current digital age, even secretaries would hardly expect to be valued for flowing script. Whilst handwritten memos may be a thing of the past, however, writing analysis is an increasingly popular way to screen job applicants.

- Unknown to many job applicants, graphology has gained surprising popularity amongst some of the top firms.
- Already extremely popular in France, the study is seen as a useful addition to other recruitment tests such as aptitude and maths.
- The UK-based Institute for Graphology find themselves in constant demand for recruitment purposes, and even the CID have used their skills.
- The science behind the art – can handwriting really tell an employer that an applicant is up to the task?

Pitch perfect

So there it is: a full pitch. The kind of thing which you'll soon be writing and sending out yourself.

Later down the line we'll come on to how to develop great pitches, brainstorm content, and identify what editors are really looking for. But for now you should be aiming to familiarise yourself with the concept of sending pitches, and why they're preferable to sending full features.

Action plan

We'll come to writing pitches later, but now you're familiar with the concept, it's important to begin practising.

1. Pick out three magazine or newspaper features which strike you as being particularly interesting ideas.

2. Write out three 'pitches' for these articles using the head-sell technique. The headline, standfirst and opening paragraph will be the same, but you'll need to fill out the bullet-pointed body of the pitch.

3. Consider from an editorial point of view how and why these pitches made it into print.

2

Knowing the market – what's out there

Freelance features in magazines and newspapers are like icebergs. Whilst effort may have gone into crafting and researching the final piece, this is nothing compared to the lengthy groundwork behind getting the initial commission. Successful freelancers spend an enormous amount of time scoping the market before making their initial approach, and in this chapter you'll discover techniques used by real freelancers to identify potential hotspots for commissions.

In this chapter, you'll:

- Gain a broad understanding of the freelance market.
- Find out where the unsold freelance hotspots are.
- Learn the signs that a publication is open to commissioning freelance writing.

If you're motivated to see yourself in print, you're probably itching to get started putting work together to send out to editors. Not so fast. Because you're about to make the classic mistake of the first-time freelancer. Lots of new writers start sending material before they've done vital initial groundwork – and it shows in the material which ends up on editors' desks. What you'll learn in this chapter is not only how to begin to do that groundwork thoroughly, but how essential it is to your future success.

Maximising your chances of success

When you're entering the magical world of the freelancer, it's easy to assume that every publication will buy in freelance work under the right circumstances. To a certain extent this is true, of course – everyone has their must-have story. But in fact the statistics are more skewed in the opposite direction.

REMEMBER: **As a rule, only one in eight publications are in the market to accept your work.**

If you look at every publication on the market today, it is the minority, not the majority, who are your potential customers. For every publication in print, slightly less than half buys in freelance work. Of this half, perhaps half again do so regularly, and half of them are open to ideas from new writers, as opposed to from their established stable of freelancers. If you do your maths, this means that about one in eight publications are worth your time submitting to.

When you first start approaching magazines with the hope of gaining freelance commissions, the natural response is to be optimistic, and to view every publication as a potential customer. There's nothing wrong with this attitude, and I have certainly got some surprising commissions from publications I thought were luke-warm about taking freelance work.

What you should always remember, though, is that whilst random pitching could work for you, it's also a sure-fire way of attracting a lot of rejection. And even if you have the self-esteem to cope with that, it's a very inefficient way of getting into print. Instead, you need to be finding out who is in the market for ideas before you pitch them.

From now on your first rule of freelancing is: *never put the idea before the market*. Before you send anything, contact anyone, or generally get carried away by your desire to be in print, you need to be asking yourself this question: "Am I putting my idea before the market?" Or, phrased in a more conventional business sense: "Is there a market for my idea?"

You might have several target publications in mind, and a head full of incredible feature ideas just waiting to jump onto the page, but approaching freelancing with what you want to see in print is completely back to front.

REMEMBER: The market comes first.

What does this mean exactly? It means that before you send anything to anyone, you first establish that there is a potential market to accept and publish your work. Otherwise you're wasting your time.

Remember that the freelance writer is a start-up company, just like any other. If you're familiar with business texts, you'll be aware of the reams of research which show how new companies soar when they've identified an opening in the market for their products. You might be smaller than other organisations by merit of being a sole trader, but the same rules apply. Any company seeking advice about how to kick-start their sales would be told by the experts in no uncertain terms that researching the market and identifying their customer base is crucial to success.

Heard of market research? Before you put pen to paper you need a thorough understanding of what's out there in the publishing world, and who is most likely to buy your ideas. The more thoroughly you scope out the market and establish the best places to sell your skills, the more payoff in the form of commissions you will receive later down the line.

The rifle, not the scattergun

Bear in mind that your resources are limited to a staff count of one, and you may well not have all the time you'd like at your disposal. So, for the reason of basic efficiency alone, you need to take the rifle rather than the scattergun approach. You simply don't have the resources at hand to send out your material to all and sundry and keep track of the results with the proper degree of effectiveness.

Many new freelancers start out with a laudable 'can do' approach. "I have ideas for lots of different publications," they might say, or "I can write for any market." This may well be the case, but when you're operating from the perspective of a small business – which is what a freelance writer is – you need to narrow your focus to optimise your limited resources.

Rather than randomly sending out your marketing materials to just anyone, you need to identify a key audience that you want to target, and tailor your work to best suit that market. Your freelance submissions are the marketing tools with which you are convincing a potential client (in this case, an editor) to buy your product – or more specifically, your writing skills. Rather than shooting out a myriad of ideas with no real idea of how they'll fit the people you're sending them to, you need to identify those few editors in the market for your work, take aim, and blow them away with your great freelance potential.

Self-esteem – your most valuable resource

Many writers start out by pitching to a lot of random people, and then suffer a blow to their confidence because of the high levels of rejection they receive. It's even something of a running joke in the writing industry that unless you receive enough rejection letters to paper your bathroom with, you're not trying.

In the media business, it's not necessary to incur this kind of excessive rejection. In fact, it means that you're not doing your research properly. More importantly, by taking a well-intentioned but disorderly approach you're squandering your most important resource – your self-esteem.

You can put yourself in line for a real crisis of confidence simply by approaching a lot of people who aren't in the market for free-lance work. When you submit your carefully crafted ideas to an editor who couldn't commission you even if they wanted to, they will most likely not take the time to explain why they don't want your work. This leads to the classic demotivating 'not for us' response. Which is not unreasonable, considering that the writer hasn't taken the time to check the market properly in the first place.

If you talk to editors, they'll tell you they receive a lot of perfectly good ideas that simply don't fit with the magazine they're working on, because writers haven't taken the trouble to examine the various sections, or to ask which are open to freelance submssions. These ideas are rejected not because they aren't any good, but because the submission doesn't address an area which needs to be filled. And although you might be ready and willing to deal with rejection, pointless rejection takes its toll on the fledgling writer, because it is limited in what it teaches you.

In the tenuous world of writing and getting published, self-belief is probably your most important resource, and you should be guarding it as carefully as possible – not squandering it on a flush of ill-planned optimism by sending your genius ideas to people who couldn't possibly commission them.

Taking the professional approach

I'm not saying you're never going to encounter rejection. But you will substantially reduce your exposure to it, and thus maximise your chances of staying motivated, when you narrow your focus to those titles which offer you a genuine chance to get into print.

Writers who have been in the business for some time tend to approach a publication knowing that there is a good possibility they will simply be striking them off the list of potentials. This isn't because the writers have become so beaten down with rejection that they can't be bothered to approach with optimism; it's simply a process of efficiency. Sending out a good pitch, as we'll come to cover, takes a lot of work both coming up with the idea and writing it specifically for a particular slot in a particular publication. Directing all that energy at an editor who is only half inclined to take ideas is a waste of effort, even if you're not planning on becoming a full-time freelancer. More importantly, squandering your energy in areas that gain you no reward is a guaranteed motivation-sapper – and motivation is what will get you into print.

The professional attitude is one which views an editor as a customer. A good salesperson doesn't bombard a customer with an item they couldn't possibly buy. Instead, they research likely customers before launching headlong into a sales pitch.

Your approach should be all about researching and targeting – not blindly contacting all and sundry.

Looking for the positive signs

So how exactly should you decide who to approach with your brilliant pitches? Generally speaking, you're looking for publications that take as high a content of freelance material as possible, to maximise an editor's need to commission. There are a number of indications that a newspaper or magazine will need a lot of freelance content.

Wrong approach	Right approach
If I send out to as many people as possible, one or two are bound to be interested – it's the law of averages.	Because print is such a competitive area, I imagine editors get lots of ill-gauged submissions. I'm going to make sure my work is personally targeted to their needs.
If at first you don't succeed – I'm going to keep trying the same editors until they buy my work.	Hounding editors isn't professional. Instead I'm going to politely check if they take freelance material before I send them anything.
I've got loads of ideas which can fit lots of different genres.	I'm going to pick a specific subject in order to capitalise on my research.
I can save myself time and get more material out there by sending the same thing to lots of different editors.	By their nature, publications usually appeal to a unique target audience. I'm going to make sure my ideas are obviously geared specifically to that readership.

- **They have a high frequency of publication.** Every month, every week, or every day is all good news for freelancers: it means that editors constantly need new material. It is hard for staff to be creative on an ongoing basis – so freelancers can be a valued source of new ideas, as well as a helping hand for staff writers.
- **They have a low staff count.** An editor who covers an entire section with no help, or who is short on sub-editors or assistants, is a good potential customer.
- **They have a lot of pages which are written by non-staff.** Check this with the editorial team for newspapers, and via the staff list at the front for magazines.
- **A lot of the same non-staff names crop up throughout.** This is a great sign. Not only do they take a lot of freelance work, but by the looks of things they're a bit limited in their choice of

freelancers. By choice, most editors would rather have a nice variety of names running through their publications, and most will avoid commissioning the same person to write several pieces for the same edition. So if you see that the same freelancer has written a number of pieces, it's a good reason to offer your fresh new ideas and writing style.

- **They require a specific or unusual area of expertise, which you happen to have.** By their nature, certain specialist subjects are less likely to have lots of people who feel confident writing about them. If you can offer an editor expertise in an area where it's hard to find, you will be an attractive option.

These are the kind of signs which should be giving you a green light to add a publication to your list of potentials. But before you get too enthusiastic, remind yourself to be ruthless about who you're ruling out.

The freelance marketplace

There might only be one in eight publications in the market to take your ideas, but don't let anyone tell you that freelancing is over-subscribed. Yes, lots of people want to do it, but not a lot of people do it well, or approach the markets which are genuinely open to commissioning writers. Take a look around your average newsagent and you'll see countless magazines, and dozens of newspapers, which run reams of material daily. Behind the scenes there are lots more publications which aren't found on the shelves for the average customer, and they also buy freelance content. There's plenty of work to go around.

Scoping for freelance potential

For the freelance feature writer, there are three main areas of potential interest. These are:

- Consumer newspapers
- Consumer magazines
- Trade publications

'Consumer' refers to publications which are usually found on newsstands and have high circulation and advertising rates. Examples include *Real Travel*, or *The Guardian*.

Trade publications are far more niche in their focus, and are generally only available by direct subscription. Titles might include *Farming Monthly*, or *British Baker Magazine*. There is some cross-over – some of the better known trades make it onto newsstands in larger retailers, and some consumer titles are quite specialist in their focus.

Each of these fields has something to offer the professional freelancer in terms of getting published and building clips. But in order to know what each might offer you when you're starting out, you need to understand a little more about the fundamentals of how the different categories use freelance material.

National newspapers

National newspapers generally have the advantages of:

- High page counts.
- Frequent turnover of copy.
- Tight deadlines and understaffing, leading to internal pressure to outsource.
- Established and generous freelance budgets.

Newspapers are a good bet for freelance writers, and here's why. They produce a huge amount of content, and are almost always understaffed. Aside from a large body of news content, newspapers usually produce at least one specialist supplement a day, which is frequently partially filled by freelancers.

Sections to aim for

When it comes to newspapers, it's actually often easier to get a commission for a full two-page feature than it is a small news piece, which looks considerably better as a clip anyway. Unless you're aiming to become a reporter, I wouldn't recommend going after the small news slots in the newspaper. They're harder than you might imagine to break into, and even if you succeed, it will only be a tiny piece and it might not even be by-lined (run with your name). With the fast-paced and pressured nature of news, editors are also more likely to rely on newswires or staff reporters for reliable fast information.

There are, however, good openings to be found in the specialist supplements which accompany daily newspapers. These sections run full features; carry specific advertising, giving them reasonable budgets; and have editors with the time and inclination to get to know new freelancers. Even better, editors usually don't ask too many questions about previous experience and clips, making them perfect for the first-time writer.

Potential problems

The problem with newspapers is that by their nature they only run very recent news content, and this tends to reflect on the features they publish. This means you need to be very aware of current events to stand a good chance of getting published regularly.

Consumer (newsstand) magazines

Consumer magazines are a good bet, in that they have:

- Steady editorial schedules, making pitching and chasing cycles easier.
- Wider scope for stories not related to breaking news, which makes pitching topics easier and your ideas less likely to date in the process.
- Established freelance slots, which makes it easier to tailor pitches in a very focused way.

Magazines are hit and miss as to whether or not they take freelance material, but their steady editorial schedules mean they usually comprise a big part of the average freelancer's income. As they tend to run monthly, there is more scope for general ideas without an up-to-the-minute news focus too, although obviously topics still reflect current trends. Most magazines put their content together at least a few months before the magazine appears on the shelves, and some file copy six months in advance.

Sections to aim for

For a freelancer, the most interesting aspect of any magazine is the 'masthead' or staff list at the front of the edition. If it only lists a handful of staff – editor, deputy and assistant, or less – then it's a good bet. Magazines with limited staff counts from small publishers are likely to take freelance material. If there is a great long list naming several sub-editors and more than one deputy editor, then you should probably rule it out.

There are exceptions. If a magazine is published frequently, such as weekly or fortnightly, there may still be openings. Also, if it runs a lot of 'real-life' stories, there will usually be a strong (and well paid) demand for these tricky-to-find case studies. It takes a certain type of person to be able to track down unusual and often traumatic incidents and then persuade the person involved to spill their guts in a national publication for a tiny or non-existent fee. But if you can do it regularly, there's good work in it.

Potential problems

For most magazines with a long staff list, however, there simply isn't the need for a freelancer's services. Or if there is, the need will be so infrequent that you're better off directing your energies at those who take regular work.

Learning the hard way: overstaffing at magazines

I worked as a deputy editor for a short time on a food magazine, which was poorly staffed and had only an editor, a food stylist and an editorial assistant working alongside me. Some recipe sections were bought in from external 'experts', as was the drink section, but the rest of the magazine was written and sub-edited (proof-read) entirely by myself, the editor and the assistant.

When it came down to it, that was only around eight features to be written and proof-read, along with the rest of the magazine content to be checked through. It wasn't a breeze, but I certainly wasn't staying late at work – so imagine how unlikely a magazine with double the staff count is to need extra help. Not to mention the fact that this kind of magazine would include assistants, work-experience staff and

---

subs who are desperate to 'break into' writing features, and regularly pitch editors from in-house. If an editor is going to hand out extra features, they'll probably field them to those in lesser staff roles. After all, these people are probably working for peanuts (and often, sadly, not being treated too well either) in the hope of gaining a few clips and working their way up into a higher position.

Trade magazines

The advantages of trade magazines are that they have:

- Great hidden potential – they're not on newsstands, so are less bombarded with freelance ideas.
- Have a very narrow focus, making it easier to tailor ideas to fit their specific audience.
- Often have surprisingly regular and reasonably paid demand for freelance submissions.
- Are more likely to have editors with the time and inclination to be courteous to freelancers.

Trade magazines are a little-known secret amongst writers, and every professional feature will almost certainly supply at least a few. The big consumer titles tend to get a lot of freelancers petitioning them for work – with good reason; they are well-known, prestigious, and of course, in easy view. It makes sense to approach them.

But there is also an enormous range of trade publications which are not found in newsagents, and are subscribed to directly by their readers. These publications cover everything from potato farming to managing a franchise business, and are aimed specifically at professions as diverse as confectionery manufacturers to HR professionals.

There are hundreds of these lesser-known titles catering to every conceivable specialism, and the best news for freelancers is they're not too well known. This means they have markedly fewer people approaching them for work, and as an extra bonus are often run on a tiny staff base and take freelance material regularly.

In addition, they usually have a well-chosen niche, ensuring them both healthy subscription rates and good advertising revenue. After all, if you sell industrial catering equipment, how else do you target an advert at your customers?

Sections to aim for

Trade publications are not too easy to find, but a few large publishing houses tend to cover dozens, so once you've tracked down one you'll usually open up quite a few titles at once. They're also much harder to get a copy of, as it's a little pushy to ask an editor to send you out an edition in the post, and their subscription rates are often expensive to reflect their specialist content. Nowadays, increasing numbers have at least some content online, but this is often in a short form to encourage subscriptions.

When you've found a publishing house which produces several trades, the best way to get hold of copies is to go into the offices and pick up a magazine in person. Magazine houses will tend to showcase copies in the reception area, and may not mind you making off with a few if you explain that you're freelance. Given that trade publications are usually part of a large company producing many titles, you can get copies of every title they produce, and even if you're not planning on pitching to all of them, obscure trades are great for brainstorming ideas.

Trade publications almost always have an editorial schedule which is published online or available from them direct. This makes it easier for freelancers to know which subjects they should be pitching in advance.

Potential problems

If you want to get a clip in a well-known title, these rather more obscure publications are probably less appealing. After all, saying that you write for *Onion Farmer Monthly* is generally less impressive than being able to claim you write for *The Guardian*, or the *New York Times*. But if you're looking to make money from freelancing as a long-term profession, then they're a good target to aim for.

A word from the editors

"Don't exclusively chase the big names. Just keep your eyes open for smaller publications. The ones that come through your door; ones you pick up in a hotel or on a train; local glossies; specialised, industry publications. Websites too. They may not all have budgets for freelance pieces, but some might and, being less inundated, they may be more receptive – especially if you have some sort of specialism or area of interest that they may not be able to cover in-house. In every case, make sure you tailor-make your pitch and show that you've read the publication."

Vicky Baker, Travel Editor, *Time Out* Publications

Other markets

There are a few other markets open to you, but I wouldn't recommend these for the beginner unless you have a particular yen or opening to approach them. These include:

Local papers

Time was when fledgling journalists would cut their teeth on local papers before moving onwards and upwards to the nationals. Nowadays, sadly, local papers seem to be a dying breed, and any movement in the market recently has been for vast swathes of them to shut down.

That's not to say they're not still a popular choice for those hoping to get into journalism – and for this reason, ironically, they're probably not worth your while as a freelance writer. Not only are freelance rates for local papers usually absolutely abysmal (we're talking rates so low that they pay by line rather than by word), but they can actually be quite tricky to get published in.

In my experience, local papers are just as difficult to freelance for as the nationals, but offer significantly less pay and prestige in the form of clips.

Online publications

This is a tricky one, as the market for online publications is undoubtedly blossoming. Newspapers are expanding their online offering and new websites running copy are starting up all the time. In general, however, clips harvested from online sources simply don't look as professional to most editors as those garnered from print media.

There are some exceptions, however, and I think it's well worth exploring these. Many newspapers and large news organisations now have a dedicated online budget, which is not as immediately obvious to new writers. This means whilst it may be quite difficult to place an article in, say, *The Guardian* travel pages, there may well be a purely online travel section. Not only will this section be open to less competition, but it will probably pay on a par with the print editions and offer up a chance to be published at a national level without the associated competition.

The same goes for large companies or web forums, such as MSN, Virgin, Yahoo! and so forth. Essentially, any organisation that sees itself as having some kind of entertainment remit may well publish features online.

But here's the bad news. Tracking down editors of web sections on enormous organisations can be very difficult. In addition, the vast majority of online publications are very poorly paid (if they pay anything at all) and, due to the nature of the media, only offer you tiny, filler-style clips.

> **Web tip:**
> It can sometimes be difficult to dig out trade magazines and online titles, as they can be quite well hidden. Logon to www.nocontacts noproblem.com/resources.html for a thorough education in tracking them down online, and a list of the large trade publishing houses.

Action plan

Now you'll begin to draw up a list of potential publications, utilising the tips in this chapter. Scout out the feature sections and supplements in newspapers which might be of interest, identify magazines with low staff counts, and track down a handful of trade publications.

1. Identify fifty publications of potential interest to you as a freelance writer.
2. Using the skills you've gained in this chapter, scan the publications for clues that they're open to freelance writers.
3. Now draw up a smaller 'hotlist' of the sections which you've identified as being amenable to commissioning freelance material, and where possible (i.e. with magazines) note down the editor or deputy editor's name and contact details.

3

Red-hot leads – narrowing your focus

By now you should have an idea that a large percentage of your work as a freelancer should include scoping the market for potential before sending your ideas. In this chapter you'll discover how to take this research process to the next level, ensuring that only red-hot leads make your final pitch list.

In this chapter you'll:

- Identify one or several specialist areas which will comprise the core of your freelance submissions.
- Discover how to turn a potential publication into a red-hot lead.
- Learn professional techniques for contacting editors.
- Understand how to read between the lines of an editor's response.

Drawing up your dynamite list of leads

Hopefully you now understand the importance of being able to rule out publications, as well as having an overview of the market. If you followed the action plan at the end of the last chapter you should also have a list of publications which show good signs of being open to freelance work.

As well as looking for people to strike off your list of potential customers, you'll now narrow your focus to ensure that the ones you're ready to pitch to are indeed good targets for your work –

and therefore represent the best odds of commissioning you. So whilst you've started off learning about how to scope the market for potential freelance spots, you'll now move up a gear and start sifting the possibilities for real openings.

Your specialist sector

Having gained a broad understanding of the kind of areas which take freelance features, and the signs which suggest that an editor is in the market for commissioning, you're ready to move to the next step of your training – deciding on your specialism.

At this stage of the process, when you're narrowing down rather than trying to pitch to all and sundry, it's wise to pick a specialist area, or a subject of expertise you plan to focus on. There are entire books written on how to specialise as a freelancer, but suffice it to say that it will help enormously if you pick a particular subject to focus on. You'll also want to ensure that your chosen subject is linked to areas which are a good bet for freelancers. This gives you the best possible chance of getting into print.

So pick a subject which is of interest to you; hopefully something you know a bit (or a lot) about already, and one that is already well represented in media. This should be a fairly broad topic – so something like business or property rather than loft-insulating or Nokia phones (although of course the latter subjects might direct you to a DIY or technology niche).

If you think you can handle the workload, you can go for more than one subject. However, for optimum results a single topic is probably best for the first-timer. It will help you maintain your focus, develop expert ideas at a good speed, and enable you to pick titles to pitch to faster, as they'll often be in the same place or with the same publisher.

I'm not an expert in anything!

Don't worry if nothing immediately leaps to mind. You don't have to be an expert in a particular field to get a commission in a national publication. Neither do you necessarily have to have really in-depth knowledge of a subject. Most journalists write on the understanding that they'll do the digging after they've gained the commission, and may develop specialist areas almost accidentally over the course of their careers. If you're unsure, just pick a subject that genuinely interests you. You're bound to learn more about it as you put your ideas together.

Subjects to avoid

I don't want to destroy anyone's dream of being a restaurant critic or travel writer, but there are some sectors which are really not advisable for the first-time writer. Certain areas have the double-whammy of being difficult to break into (by merit of being the kind of thing everyone wants to write about) and of being a non-specialist subject – such as 'food' or 'women's issues'.

So whilst you might fancy travel as an area of expertise, it's worth bearing in mind that this is an area which has every student, backpacker, retired person and general holiday-maker pitching their ideas to national broadsheets.

That's not to say you should absolutely rule it out. If you've extensive experience of travelling, and read travel magazines and newspaper supplements religiously, you might consider this your area of expert knowledge. After all, whilst editors of travel pages get a lot of pitches, that's not necessarily to say they get a lot of good ones which are professionally put together. So if you have a number of really engaging travel ideas which you know have never run before, then feel free to pitch. But I can virtually guarantee you that you'll get into print faster with a different subject.

Generally, though, the purpose of this book is to let you know what you're up against so that you can pick the spots most likely to take on your work. I'd be doing you a disservice if I didn't point out that pitching your work to the travel section of a national paper is putting yourself up against literally thousands of competitors every time you pitch. Even professional freelance travel writers don't usually gain most of their work from the nationals – they're just too oversubscribed.

What is advisable is to begin picking your niche strategically for a subject most likely to see you in print. Then, once you've got those valuable clips and experience under your belt, you can always get started on moving across to a different subject.

Undersold subject areas

For most first-timers, the sensible thing to do is increase your odds of being noticed by aiming for sections which have fewer writers approach them. Sadly, this does often mean subjects which are perceived as being quite dry or boring – money or technology, for example. But approaching these sections also means a much higher chance of seeing your work in a national publication quickly, which is exciting.

Certain subjects also attract more people wishing to place advertising in the relevant supplement or magazine. This means that there are generally more pages to fill, and more publications in print in these areas. It therefore makes sense to pick them out as your specialism; not only is there more space to accommodate your work, but you can easily re-jig ideas on the same subject and send them to different magazines. So with minimal reworking, an idea on employment, for example, could fit into a careers section, or into a magazine for HR staff.

Subject areas I would recommend for the first-timer as being heavy on pages, budgets, and freelance space are:

- Money/personal finance
- Technology
- Education
- Real life
- Careers/jobs
- Property

Not the most interesting subjects in the world – although real life could be, if you're willing to track down and interview people with juicy stories to tell. But these are subject areas with real potential for a novice freelancer to break into a national newspaper, or a consumer magazine. Coincidentally, they're also usually well paid for freelance jobs, which is another good reason to go after them.

The viability of these subjects will also change depending on economic circumstances, so be aware of that too. Job sections often take a bit of a tumble during a recession, whilst personal finance sections hold steady or even increase. Boom times will see plenty of jobs pages and property pages spring up.

As the next part of your training process, you should now be looking to identify some key markets for your ideas which could work as your particular niche. For newspaper pitches I would suggest that you spend some time reading every newspaper every day of every week to identify which supplements go out on which days. Then narrow down the supplements you think you could pitch some good ideas to by subject, and read a few back issues of those supplements to get a feel for their content.

Narrowing your focus

Finding the right slot for your specialism

Even when you've picked out the section you'll be pitching to, there's still some narrowing down to do. Whilst it's tempting to pitch to an entire magazine or supplement, it's usually better to aim for just one or two slots which you know are freelance. This means paying attention to the way in which the publication is structured, reading the headings at the top of the pages, and noting a particular page where your work will fit.

The other reason for targeting your spot so specifically is that it allows you to find out exactly where a publication places freelance work. Whilst an editor might say quite correctly that their publication accepts freelance material, this doesn't always pertain to every aspect of the magazine or supplement. In fact, several parts may be written by in-house staff or by a freelancer who is always commissioned to write that slot. So you could be sending your work to a magazine with a vague idea that it will fit their opinion pages, only to discover that this particular area is never covered by freelancers.

> *Learning the hard way: checking the section*
> *I once pitched to a travel magazine which the editor assured me was more or less all open to freelance. But when I mentioned a particular slot at the front of the magazine, he explained that section was all written in-house. If I hadn't asked, I may well have wasted my time pitching for that section. And it goes without saying you don't want to spend your time putting together pitches for sections which can't receive them.*

Publication formats

Generally speaking, with some simple research you can tell quite easily which sections of newspapers and magazines are closed to freelancers. If you get hold of a few back editions of a magazine you're interested in pitching to, and which you know accepts free-lance, you'll notice from the contents page that it is written to a very deliberate format.

So a food title, for example, will usually have a certain number of pages dedicated to short, filler-style news items with pictures; a certain number of recipe pages which will be written by their own staff or food stylists; and perhaps some other pages written every edition by some sort of specialist. Obviously, none of these sections is really open to freelance submissions, and, whilst the filler pages can be an 'in' of sorts, they are usually reserved for junior staff to write. Besides, wouldn't you prefer to write and get paid for full features?

The sections left over may or may not be open to freelance, but you can check (and impress an editor with your knowledge of his or her publication at the same time) by asking specifically about a section by title.

If you're looking at a magazine rather than a newspaper, you can also use this straightforward method of investigating a particular section:

1. Identify the section you're interested in writing for.
2. Read the standfirst above the feature or features in that section. The standfirst (otherwise known as the byline) is the little line of text leading into the piece.
3. Check the writer's name against the staff list at the front of the publication.
4. If the author isn't mentioned as an employee (or is put in the section labelled 'contributors'), then they're freelance. This probably means that the section accepts freelance work, and you can go ahead and pitch for it.

The exception to this rule would be if the same freelancer wrote that same slot every edition. This does sometimes happen, so check a few back copies if you can. If there's no name at all on the standfirst, it's written in-house. That doesn't mean it can never take freelance ideas, but will give you a clue as to how to phrase your questioning when you're talking to the editor ("I notice such and such section has been written by staff for the last few editions – do you ever use freelancers here?").

With newspapers the structures in place are generally less rigid, as pages tend to be more reactive to occurring news rather than delivering content in a formatted style. This means that there is usually scope for freelance on a lot more pages of a section too. But again, check before you pitch.

REMEMBER: **Random enthusiasm doesn't work. Pick your niche strategically.**

You may be thinking at this stage that such an involved approach sounds a bit tedious. A few articles in print is all you're after, and developing a specialist subject area before you've even sent an idea out is a bit too career-heavy for what you had in mind.

But if you're serious about getting something into print – even if you don't want to freelance for a living – specialising and targeting is the *fastest way to get published*. If you're just testing the waters, it's tempting to send out a few submissions or call a few editors blindly and see what bites. Unfortunately, you should know that this kind of random enthusiasm is a lengthy approach at best, and totally useless at worst.

Adopting the professional approach is the most efficient way to get your work published. You might use a strategy of sending out ideas to absolutely everyone you can think of, and by sheer luck and big numbers it could eventually pay off with a commission. But it is an enormous expense of energy, and a much longer route. And you're interested in the fastest way – right?

A word from the editors

"Make sure you pitch to the correct section editor (where relevant) and SPELL THEIR NAME RIGHT! Also, make sure that you tailor your pitch to a specific section of the magazine, which saves the editor time. Relevance is absolutely crucial – when I was at Wallpaper* a writer pitched me a rugby tour idea (it's a design and lifestyle glossy) and recently I had a Yemen pitch for easyJet Traveller... Not great."

Jeroen Bergmans, Editor, *easyJet Inflight Magazine*

Effort now means pay-off later

The other reason for this exacting approach in the early stages is that it has multiple pay-offs in terms of saving you time later down the line. When you identify a particular subject to focus your efforts on, you'll turn up a lot of interesting ideas which you can rework and resend to a number of different slots. If however you start casting about for 'good ideas' and send them to a number of niche areas, you'll lose this crucial time-saver later down the line. And as you'll find out, saving yourself extra effort in the pitching process is worth some initial work.

Before you send anything out to anyone, you need to establish that:

- **The publication buys freelance work.** In the rush of writing enthusiasm, this is easy to overlook. You may have a favourite magazine which you're just dying to get published in, or an idea you know would make a great story. But if they don't buy freelance work, they don't buy freelance work – no matter how appealing your pitch.

- **The editor is currently in the position to buy freelance work.** Budgets change, editors get overloaded, and publishers put a block on freelance. All of these things occur regularly, so make sure you find out that's not the situation at the publication you're about to spend your precious time submitting to.

- **They buy freelance work regularly enough for you to get a look-in.** Several features once a month is good; a dozen every week is great. Play the odds, and don't waste your time on a magazine that has twenty or more writers wrestling over one monthly slot.

Contacting the editors

Establishing that work is available

So how do you make sure that an editor is wide-open to your ideas? We've already covered some techniques to determine whether or not a publication is *likely* to buy freelance work, and this information should have informed your growing list of publications you plan to pitch to.

But from that list of 'maybes' we now want to extract the hottest leads, and the best way to do this is quite simply to call and ask. When it comes to establishing for certain whether an editor is going to take even a passing interest in something you send in, a direct conversation with the person in charge is the only way forwards.

Remember the 'No Contacts' philosophy? You're aiming to behave with confidence and professionalism at all times, and sending an email (or worse, a letter) asking whether an editor is in line for your work is neither confident nor professional. Instead, you'll need to take a deep breath and phone the publication you're considering sending your ideas to.

In doing so you not only save yourself time, you also identify the best possible person to send ideas to in the process, get their contact details, and (hopefully) gain an advantage before you pitch by sounding like a competent professional over the phone. Then when you send your ideas through, you can allude to the conversation, and the editor should remember you as that professional person from the earlier phone call.

Talking to the right person

Ensuring that you're talking to the person who actually commissions is also very important. People don't tend to like to reject enthusiastic freelancers, so you may find yourself talking to another staff member who will encourage you to send something in. If you get through to an editor who is not commissioning, however, they will rarely want to make more work for themselves by suggesting you send them writing they can't use.

You should have a name for an editor before you call, but in some circumstances, such as with newspaper supplements, you might have to ask. Some magazines have an editor, a deputy and a features editor, so it makes sense to double-check which one should be receiving your submissions. If it's not obvious who does what, just confirm with whoever you're speaking to that you want to talk to 'the person who commissions freelance writers'.

Learning the hard way: talking to the commissioning editor
I had an experience where I phoned to ask about a small section at the front of a weekly magazine which came with a well-known newspaper. The staff member I spoke to said that the section was written solely by freelancers, which seemed to me the perfect opportunity to send my work in. It was a very small slot, so rather than pitch an idea I lovingly crafted a short piece out in full and sent it off.

A few chase-ups later and I got through to the person actually in charge of commissioning, who told me that whilst it was written by freelancers, they relied solely on the skills of a pre-ordained group which they were not looking to expand. The experience certainly taught me to really cement whether or not an editor takes freelance.

The initial phone call

It's quite natural to be nervous when calling an editor to ask about freelancing – and, without meaning to, to heap further stress on the situation. This is the exact point where sounding calm and collected can make all the difference to your chances. Almost all freelancers sound a little nervy when phoning up about their work, so if you come across as assured and forthright, an editor will usually assume that you've been in the business a while.

A good tip is to stand up whilst you're on the phone – it deepens your voice and makes you feel naturally more authoritative. You may also find you feel more comfortable playing the freelance role with only the editor as an audience. So pick a private spot where there's no-one listening in.

To give you an idea of the best approach, a phone call might go something like this:

"Hello, my name's [your name]. I'm a freelance writer and I was thinking of sending you through some ideas. But I just wanted to call and check if you're in the market for freelance work at the moment."

This covers most bases, so that if an editor is short on budget, full-up with commissioned features, or simply doesn't and never will take freelance, they can now fill you in. If an editor gives you the green light to send ideas, it's also usually sensible to clarify which sections or areas they might be most open to receiving pitches for, without sounding pushy, desperate, or like you don't know what you're doing. So you might say something like:

"OK, that's great. I'll put some ideas together for you. Are there any particular areas which you find you're particularly short on ideas for?"

The response to this question is usually about 70% of editors saying "no, nothing in particular". But to me it's well worth asking for the 30% or so of editors who will fill you in on areas they find hard to get good ideas for. Or those who will give you valuable information about the type of feature they want.

If you've managed to find an editor who claims to be in the market for ideas, *and* has an area they have difficulties getting good ideas for, then that's gold-dust for a freelancer. You've not only identified an opening for your work, but you've even given yourself a better chance of your ideas being looked upon favour-ably because they cater to an area which is low on ideas or material.

Danger signs

There are also some danger signs you can pick up over the phone, to indicate that you shouldn't bother pitching. They might not deter you completely, but they should at least save you some time crafting a pitch dedicated solely to that publication. When you pick up the phone, you might hear one of these discouraging responses:

"We don't really take freelance except in exceptional cases. But I'd be happy to see some of your ideas."

For this, read – "I don't want to reject you outright, and we took a celebrity feature two years ago which we couldn't cover in-house, but otherwise everything is written by staff". Most people are nice. They don't want to tell someone 'no' or 'never'. But as a freelancer you have to work out the gigs which are worth your time pursuing. Be firm, if you like, and ask more questions: "How often do you take freelance?" is a good one. Generally, though, I'd write this one off and move on.

"All of our freelancers have to write something on spec for us in the first instance."

This doesn't happen very often, and it's usually the case with large magazines with big budgets (who are not your best targets anyway). If it does happen, my advice would be not to bother. Essentially it means that they're not treating you with professional courtesy and recognising you as the skilled writer you are. In my experience, a publication that behaves in this way from the outset follows right through with this behaviour to the point where they discard your carefully written on-spec piece as being not quite right.

(Sounding doubtful) "We don't take much freelance work."

Funnily enough, you shouldn't necessarily rule this one out. I've had a few editors say this to me and then go on to take ideas on a monthly basis. So it may be worth your while giving it a go.

"We don't have much of a budget for freelance work. But if you're happy to work for lower rates, I can look at your ideas."

Move on. A publication that isn't prepared to pay professional rates isn't worth bothering with. Neither is it good for your fellow writers to encourage this disreputable behaviour. When a magazine or newspaper is paying considerably below par, they really shouldn't be in business: they can't muster the funds to pay their staff properly, and this deficit will come over in all kinds of other ways. Publications which do this often go on to ask all kinds of other unreasonable requests for the pittance they're paying, and are never a good enough name to make it worthwhile gaining clips, either. Have respect for yourself as a professional, and find a proper outlet for your work.

> *"We have a list of freelancers. Send me your details and I'll put you on file."*

Don't bother. As silly as this sounds for something which will take you a minute in an email, it's a waste of your time. In ten years I have never, never, ever, not once been contacted by a publication that has 'found' me in their files. In this circumstance, send pitches tailored to the publication, or nothing at all.

Asking your own qestions

There are key questions which will help you get to the heart of whether a magazine really is in the market for your work. Here are a few you might want to try:

- Is most of your material written in-house?
- Do you have a budget for freelance work?
- Do you often commission freelance work?
- Do you have a lot of freelancers who send you ideas?

And, once you've established that they have work:

- Are there any particular areas you have difficulty covering?
- Do you have a lot of writers who pitch on a similar subject?
- Is now a good time to send you ideas?
- Could you let me know what part of the month you go to press in? I'd like to avoid sending ideas when you're busy.
- Which particular section/pages are open to freelance work?
- Is the ..... section written in-house, or is it freelance?

Obviously you wouldn't want to ask an editor all of these questions in one phone call! But they can help you to focus your pitch, whilst demonstrating your professionalism and commitment to research.

Other good questions for magazines

Magazines are different from newspapers in that they can plan their issues a long time in advance of the press date. In fact, for the first-time writer it's often quite staggering how long a publication will leave between the time they write the issue and the month it's actually on the shelves for purchase.

Different publications, however, will have different schedules, and whilst a few will only have a month or so 'lead' time, the majority have three – and an occasional publication has up to six. So a very good question to ask is: "What edition are you currently working on?" Armed with that information, you can time your ideas to fit with the month in which the next issue hits the shelves.

Another peculiarity of some magazines is that they plan all their content literally a whole year in advance, with very little room for variation. This may be off-putting for the new freelancer who sees that all the idea slots have been covered, but in fact, you can often get into print this way by pitching a good angle on a planned idea. Magazines which have this habit publish editorial schedules which are publicly available to advertisers (and writers). For magazines, then, another good question is: "Do you have an editorial schedule, or do you plan your sections on a monthly basis?"

Note that magazines in the latter camp will usually tell you, very proudly, that all their fresh content is dreamed up every month by staff in special meetings. In the case of the former, they can often send you a copy, or it may well be on their website.

Web tip:
Narrowing your focus gets easier the more you practise, and it always helps to receive feedback from editors. You can also read up on a slew of great editors' tips at
www.nocontactsnoproblem. com/editorstips.html

Action plan

You should now start to spend some time on the telephone, calling a range of publications from nationals to trades, and identifying a list of what you consider to be prime targets for your material.

1. From your earlier list of potential publications, ring all the editors or deputies using the tips in this chapter.

2. Match their responses to those we've covered, and use your own intuition to work out which are likely to be worth your time pitching to.

3. Jot down some notes, based on facts you've picked up from speaking to the editors about which subjects/angles are most likely to be of interest to them.

4

Not so fast! Before you pitch

Nearly there! We're not quite at the pitching stage yet, but almost. This chapter will help you fine-tune what makes a good pitch great, and ensure that you're sending only top-quality news fodder to the most likely candidates.

In this chapter, you'll:

- Understand what makes a good pitch great.
- Learn how to refine your idea to perfectly fit an editor's needs.
- Find out the pitching mistakes to avoid.

Now that you've got your great ideas and target editors lined up, you must be aching to get some of your raw talent across to them. But before you reach that point, there is some more work to be done. A common mistake for first-time writers is to run away with the importance of good ideas. Now, don't get me wrong: good ideas are not only important, they are essential to landing a freelance commission. But they're not the be all and end all. And no idea, no matter how brilliant, will fit in a publication for which it's not correctly tailored.

So whilst your first arm of research was discovering whether a particular publication has openings for a freelance writer, your second crucial approach is to write an idea that the editor can imagine seeing in print.

Once you've sifted the market for potential openings, and hopefully established at least a few good bets, it's time to move to the next level. At this stage you've reached the part of your training which will form the heart of your future freelancing, and will be the crux of whether or not you get into print.

Now it's time to take all those good leads, and to start converting them into possible commissions – by crafting ideas for editors. We'll work on exactly what you should be sending in, and the crucial criteria which editors look for when they consider buying-in freelance work.

The three elements of a winning pitch

In order of priority, the three elements which make up a pitch that sells are:

- **The idea exactly fits the publication** – trickier, and more work than it sounds. Your idea must be directly pitched at a slot which the magazine fills with freelance material.
- **You've identified a great idea** – one which is fresh, original, hasn't been covered anywhere else and preferably picks up on some current trend or news.
- **It's well-written** – the most obvious of points, and down to your own innate talents.

Evidently, a good pitch is one which gets commissioned. But there are some very important elements to a good pitch, and in terms of priority, first-time writers often get these wrong. Not unreasonably, new players tend to presume it is the calibre of their writing which will get their pitch noticed and commissioned. Not so.

In fact, if you've picked up a magazine or newspaper recently you'll notice that a fine literary style is not what makes a good feature. You might admire the fine working of a clever headline, but ultimately it is something more compelling that moves you to read a piece in a daily newspaper. If you study the text of many tabloids, a pedant might even argue that it is actually *badly* written. But most daily newspapers would agree that it's better for their sales to run with a great story than to polish some less interesting news to a high literary shine. Don't get me wrong – you do need to be able to write well to get in print. But don't run away with the idea that it is your genius at wordplay which will lift your pitches above the masses an editor receives.

Next up is the assumption that it is good ideas which set professional writers apart from the amateurs. Well, this is partially true: great ideas are what editors want to buy-in for their publications, and if you can present them with one they just can't bear to pass up, then this will go a long way towards getting your piece into print.

But long before an editor judges your idea as genius or your writing style as appealing, they'll be looking to see that what you've sent *exactly fits their publication*. This is what will ultimately drive an editor to genuinely consider an idea, before they think through other aspects of your ability. So once again, in order of importance, a winning pitch:

1. Fits the publication it's aimed at.
2. Covers a great idea.
3. Is well written.

Having addressed these key points, hopefully you now understand in more detail why the earlier 'groundwork' chapters are so essential to your future success. If your enthusiasm to find out about pitching has moved you to skip straight to this section, go back and read the first three chapters now.

Stretching to fit – making your pitch fit the market

You'll remember from Chapter 1 that the most important thing a pitch must have is the potential to fit the publication you're pitching it to. This might sound pretty obvious, but it's more tempting than you realise, when you've hit upon what you think is a killer idea, to hope that an editor will share your thoughts and find a space for it.

REMEMBER: **If you don't keep reminding yourself that publications are rigid in structure and coverage, your rejected pitches will do the job for you.**

Magazines and newspapers have strictly delineated sections, and they only fill those sections with the topics which have been pre-ordained by the team or the publisher – or whoever has the decision-making power. They do this because this is how successful advertising strategies are formulated, which is how they make their profit.

Learning the hard way: advertising versus editorial

Many big magazines have more people selling advertising than they do on the editorial team, and they make more money from the adverts than they do from the cover price. I once worked for a magazine whose editor routinely boasted that their sales were so high that the cover-price revenue was outdoing the advertising. What this should have communicated very strongly to the publisher is that the magazine wasn't selling enough adverts to stay in business, and in fact the publication folded only a few months later.

On the flipside of that, the publisher of The Star *is often criticised for ploughing all of his energies into generating the advertising side of his newspaper above the editorial content. But he is still in business, making very high profits and keeping his editorial team in wages. The moral of the story is that whilst it's nice to strike a balance, most publications are to a lesser or greater extent looking to commission things which satisfy their advertisers and sell space. A newspaper will run a motoring supplement, say, in order to sell adverts to car companies. So even if you have a brilliant story on caravans, it won't make it in if no caravan companies have expressed an interest in buying space.*

Fitting your pitch to a particular section doesn't just cover the idea or how's it's angled. It also comes down to how you write your head-sell – in some detail. If you're approaching a travel magazine which only prints first-person features, don't write your pitch in the third person. If you're pitching a tabloid, your writing style must be 'tabloidese'.

This might sound obvious, but once you get into the hard work of sending out your brilliant pitches, it's tempting to look at a well-written pitch which is not *quite* in the style of the particular publication, and hope the editor will recognise the potential.

But ultimately you're the professional here, so your job is to make life as easy as possible for the editor. Don't ask them to use their imaginations, and don't expect them to recognise the raw talent or literary brilliance of a pitch which doesn't fit their publication. Because they won't – and nor should they.

Your job as freelancer – provide the imagination

Have you ever watched those TV programmes which show buyers how to decorate their homes for sale? The key message of the experts in these programmes is 'buyers have no imagination' – it's up to the house-seller to present their property in a way that the prospective buyer can imagine themselves living in it.

The print media world is no different. If your idea is not written *exactly* as it could appear in the newspaper or magazine, an editor won't imagine it any different. Nor will they commission it with the proviso that it's reworded. It's not an editor's job to train writers to supply them with freelance content which fits their publication. It's up to the freelancer to pitch in a way to make it immediately obvious that their idea is the perfect fit.

Your pitch *must look like something which the editor already has in print* in their section or magazine. So you need to examine not only the kinds of ideas which a section runs, but the style in which they are written too. This isn't the time to go maverick with your literary writing style or off-the-wall interpretation of a newspaper feature. Make it compelling by all means, but keep it in line with the others in that publication.

Before you do anything else, your main job is to research carefully the type of freelance articles which make it into the publication you're aiming for, and to make your pitch echo the style. This comes down to ideas which would fit, but also the way in which pieces are normally written, which can be more subtle than you realise.

Here's an example of two potential introductions for a travel publication pitch.

Introduction one

"May I remind you all that the speaking of Spanish is absolutely prohibited," says our host Alvoro, as we board the bus in Madrid.

From here it's a two-hour journey north to a Spanish region where English is the official language. Once deserted, the tiny village of Valdelavilla is now owned by a forward-thinking language school. English speakers are invited to stay for free – provided that they're willing to share their company with Spanish residents.

Introduction two

The deserted Spanish hamlet of Valdelavilla has finally been repopulated. But it's not Spanish voices that ring thorough the quaint cobbled streets. In fact the native tongue is expressly forbidden here. The small collection of rustic stone properties is now owned by a forward-thinking language school. And English speakers are invited to stay for free – provided that they're willing to share their company and conversation with Spanish residents.

You might have a preference for one of these introductions, or you might not. But either of these could be right for one publication and wrong for another. The magazine which goes for the kind of edgy, first-person approach of the first would never go for the second. Whilst more middle-of-the-road publications which never write from the first-person perspective would be likely to commission the second.

In theory they might both like the *idea*. But how it is packaged to them will be crucial to its likelihood of getting into print. Writing a pitch which is *exactly* like the kind of features they already have published is what will get your pitch considered – with the difference being, of course, that your idea will be new and compelling.

Rough diamonds

Because a pitch is not a finished article, some kindly editors may say that they don't necessarily expect it to be perfectly grammatically finished and consistent with their publication style. But when it comes down to what they actually commission, it's a different story.

When you're starting out in particular, you should be aiming for the highest possible standard, because, to put it bluntly, you've little else to recommend you. So pay a lot of attention to detail in the grammar and layout of your pitch.

Once you've established a relationship with an editor, you actually have a bit more leeway on this, as they generally understand that the pitch is a rough working of how the piece will look, rather than a finished document. I've actually (embarrassingly) submitted pitches with typos right in the opening paragraph which have nevertheless been commissioned, but I wouldn't want to make a habit of it. As a writer you're being paid partly for your creative flair, but also for your accuracy and attention to detail in turning out copy. Few editors would look favourably on a writer who can't even keep a small paragraph error-free.

In terms of content, all editors are different in what they look for in a pitch from a new writer. In factual pieces such as the 'head-sell' pitch outlined in the first chapter, you'll probably want to refer to the people you'll be calling upon to add factual quotes to your article. In this respect some editors are interested in what 'names' and experts you plan to use as commentary, whilst others are happy just to see a brief overview of what you might cover. As an editor gets to know you better, they usually don't need to see every potential expert named in the piece. And a lot of editors aren't so bothered that you say specifically who you will use to talk in the piece – just the word 'expert' is fine.

The perfect head-sell

In my experience the beauty of the 'head-sell' pitch format is that if you start with a really juicy intro, the person reading it really wants to know what happens next. At this point you've already sold your piece, and the bullet points can give a fairly rough outline of where you'll go with the content.

If you're going for the most professional pitch you can possibly put together (and for your first pitch, why wouldn't you?), then do the whole lot – go with a great opening paragraph and bullet points which outline in detail exactly who you'll be talking to.

I also find that including a proper headline and stand-first increases the chances of selling your pitch. Yes, it's more work – but if you present the opening of a piece exactly how it will look in the magazine or newspaper, it helps an editor to imagine it in their publication.

Using experts in your pitch

The people you identify as your 'experts' should obviously be well qualified to talk about the area you're writing about. But here's the thing – you really don't need to worry too much about getting their permission or checking their availability before pitching. If you do that, you'll never get enough pitches out of the door to secure work. Your primary goal is to get a commission; once you've done that, then you can start worrying about who to schedule in for interviews. If you don't use the exact same expert you mentioned in a pitch, but you use someone in an identical area with a similar job title, no editor will mind. Unless, of course, you've named some kind of celebrity, in which case the commission may count strongly on your fulfilling the promise to get quotes from this person. But otherwise don't worry about it too much.

The pitch doesn't have to be one hundred percent how you would write it, either. After all, it's a pitch – an outline of what you'll write. Firstly there's a strong chance that some of that will change once you start researching in more detail. And what's more, many editors will commission an article based on a pitch, but give you their own outline of what they'd like covered.

Mistakes to avoid

You're the professional here, so it's your job to study the market and discover what kind of things the readers are likely to be interested in. But you're also offering a service – a research service if you will, in that you're researching the subject on the editor's behalf to tell them what's new. This means that you should be careful of the following.

Pitching an idea which has already run
You'd be surprised how often this happens, although it may not be the end of the world. Most editors aren't so egotistical that they expect you to memorise the content of their entire back issue for the past six months. But a word of caution – some do, and the ones most likely to be guilty of this are on the big-name magazine titles.

At worst, this situation is slightly embarrassing, but at least it means you're on the right track. Avoid this happening where possible, however, by reading a few back issues or searching the publication content online. You could even phone a junior staff member and ask them whether a similar story has run, if you want to be ultra-cautious.

Actually, some editors may even be a little impressed if you pitch something they've run in the last year, as it shows you're on the money for the type of content they favour. But you should definitely make sure that you avoid pitching something in an edition which is currently in print – that's just careless.

Pitching the wrong style to the wrong publication

Mainly, this takes the form of pitching an idea to a trade magazine in a consumer style, although it could also happen the other way around. This mistake is the most common amongst new writers who are often in love with the style of the consumer magazine and write with that in mind.

Trade editors are understandably touchy about this. Their titles tend to be *very* specifically tailored to a particular interest, and the last thing they want is light pieces aimed at a general public which only have a slight nod to their target audience. Not to mention the fact that it rather draws attention to your mind being on the glory of prestigious consumer titles rather than the lowly trade arena in which they've ended up. Show them that you understand their readership by pitching with them in mind, and they'll love you for it.

Pitching an idea which is generic and/or 'old news'

Just because an idea *could* run in a publication doesn't give an editor the impetus to pay good money for it. Your ideas need to be above the standard of the editorial brainstorming meeting to get a look-in, and they need to show a real understanding of and insight into the subject you're tackling.

You're particularly vulnerable to this mistake if you're writing on a subject you don't know too much about. In such instances you should check, as far as possible, whether a subject which seems fresh and exciting is actually old hat.

An example of a bad pitch in this respect might be suggesting a piece on 'finding a good savings account' to a money section, or 'landing your ideal job' to a careers supplement. These ideas could probably run in the relevant sections, and are likely to be covered on an annual basis in line with some supplement. But a publication will have more than enough bored staffers to cover such tired topics, or an editor with a wealth of experience who could trot it out in an hour and a half.

A word from the editors

"When pitching ideas, let the editor know why you are the right person to write the piece. If you have a particular interest in a topic, or experience related to it, that will always show through and make the piece more interesting. Include why you think the article is timely, and how it relates to what is going on in the world about which you want to write."

Victoria Ward, Editor, *Fortnum & Mason Magazine*

Professionalism – it's a state of mind

Before we get to the next chapter, where you'll be moving into the active process of pitching, it's time for a recap of what makes a good freelancer. Remember the watchwords from the beginning of the book?

REMEMBER: **Confidence, professionalism and determination.**

Believe it or not, good freelancing is as much about emotional intelligence as it is about talent. Many capable individuals with superb writing skills and great ideas are unable to get into print because they lack either confidence or basic abilities in professional conduct.

So this is the stage where you should be psyching yourself up to put your best foot forward. It is absolutely essential that you do *not* see yourself as an outsider, an amateur, a student, a work experience, or any other lowly position. By merit of putting good ideas together and sending them out to the relevant people you *are* a freelance writer – even if you haven't been commissioned yet.

Don't discount this statement as some kind of word trickery. It's absolutely true. When you're pitching to editors, you are on exactly the same level as freelancers who have been in the business for five or ten years or more. You are judged more or less solely on the quality of your writing, and even professionals who are years into their careers approach new editors from exactly the same standpoint as you.

Obviously, it does help if you're an established name on the freelance circuit with a definite specialism for which editors recognise you. At the very least your writing will probably be under less scrutiny. But there are plenty of successful freelancers who are not well known throughout the industry by name. And in fact, once they move out of their specialist sector, even established writers usually drop back to the level of the unknown. So a freelance food writer writing across major consumer titles and well known for their expertise in a particular area would be unlikely to be a recognised name in travel, for example, and certainly not in highly divergent areas like money or property.

Approach with confidence

Remember that you are equal to most other freelancers who approach an editor – even if you're not in print yet. And an editor certainly won't know that you're not in print somewhere. With the number of magazines and other literary sources out there, it would be impossible to discount the fact that someone had been published nationally unless you were gifted with some kind of print-media omnipotence.

Of course there's a big difference between knowing that this is the case, and feeling like a professional when you approach an editor. In fact, if you ask those who have been writing for a long time, many still feel like they're on the outside sometimes. But when you talk to an editor on the phone and approach them in writing, everything about your manner should suggest that you have plenty of experience and that you *are* a professional writer.

Easier said than done, admittedly. After all, most freelancers begin work as an assistant or work experience, and work their way up over a course of years to editorial roles – from whence they jump into freelancing with a number of contacts, first-hand experience of the print-media world, and most importantly, confidence in their ability to write and pitch ideas to a national standard.

What you're going to do is launch yourself straight onto this level, without the years of slog in between. And that certainly takes self-confidence. For the most part, however, plenty of practice picking up the phone, pitching ideas and chasing them up is the most direct route to believing in yourself as a writer. Not least because you'll be getting high-speed feedback and conducting your own training. If you're phoning people up and telling them you're a freelance writer several times a day, it's only natural that you will come to believe it yourself. Which is another good reason to get on the phone and start researching the best markets for your ideas.

Believe in yourself

So be the character. View it as an acting role if you must, but never apologise for contacting an editor, or act like they're doing you a favour by looking over your ideas. I'm not implying that you should behave in an arrogant or rude way. The editor is the customer, after all, and must be treated with professional courtesy at all times. But don't forget that you are offering them a service, and an attractive one at that. A good freelancer can breathe life into the features list of a publication, save the staff plenty of time working on pieces, maximise the efficiency of editorial schedules, and help add colour and good writing to a publication. So don't underestimate your potential importance.

Even if you only want one article published for posterity, the key to getting your work into print is to act like this is your business. Editors will pick up on your tone and assume that you know what you're doing (which you do). Calling in a nervous, apologetic manner, however, will tend to make anyone suspicious about your experience and value to their organisation. So stand up tall, speak clearly, and sound like the confident professional writer you are.

> **Web tip:**
> If you're still not quite sure what makes a great pitch, logon to the website to access a stack of great pitches and remind yourself of what defines a winning story: www.nocontactsnoproblem.com/pitches.html

Action plan

You should now have a reasonable list of leads from editors you have spoken to. Based on these openings, it's now time to start formulating pitches with these targets in mind.

1. Read through your list of notes on editors' responses, and decide which ones seemed the most intimidating.

2. Now formulate pitches for those least favourite areas, ensuring that you stick with the tips for high-quality pitches given in this chapter.

3. Reread these pitches, imagine the least approachable editor's response to them, and rework them again if necessary – to the highest possible standard.

5

Ready ... set ... pitch!

Congratulations! You're nearly halfway through, and you now know more about the fundamentals of freelancing than many who have been in the business for years. Don't underestimate how important these foundations are to this next chapter, which is all about pitching.

In this chapter, you'll:

- Discover more about what makes an idea that an editor wants to buy.
- Learn some different methods for writing pitches.
- Find out the best way to get your ideas to editors.
- Start sending out your own pitches.

The ideas factory – what makes a saleable feature?

So you've done your research and nailed your target markets, and you're ready to send your first pitch. The good news is that you've already done a lot of the hard work. Not only that, but you've completed groundwork which most self-starters don't usually realise needs to be done. As a reader of published material you'll have seen how only a small proportion of work is represented in a finished article, but now you know that majority of the effort needed to get something in print happens long before the commission.

At this stage you'll want to sit down with a pen and paper, or perhaps in front of your computer with Internet access, to investigate your ideas further and improve pitches you're already working on. Before you start, run your mind back over our three golden rules of what makes a good pitch:

1. **It fits the publication it's aimed at.**
2. **It covers a great idea.**
3. **It's well written.**

Good ideas

As we've discussed, editors who commission freelance work are in the business of buying ideas, rather than writing. For the most part they'll have a whole team of staff who can write for them, not to mention their own abilities in this field. They commission things they can't cover themselves, either because they haven't thought of them and are looking for fresh insights, or because you offer some kind of expertise that isn't readily available.

Ideally, of course, you'll have both, and if you have some kind of expertise I would recommend you use it to get started. If you're talented enough to have a law degree or to have spent ten years in the medical profession, you'll have a valuable leg-up into one of these specialist sectors. Once you've got going you can look to jump into different areas if that's your preference.

Here is the best tip I ever had on identifying whether an idea is worth pitching: "**Either pitch something which is going to ground, or a new take on an old idea.**" In other words, pick up on a trend which hasn't been covered, or address an old topic in a really refreshing way. Beyond that, there's not much else to it, besides your own determination to hunt out newsworthy stories and an awareness for knowing the kind of features your chosen publication tends to run. The latter is a learned skill, so don't worry if you're not immediately on the money: you'll pick it up.

REMEMBER: **It's one thing to write up an idea which could feature in a particular publication; it's another to have an idea so compelling that an editor is moved to buy it from an outside source.**

If you have no particular expertise to recommend you – and I didn't – you can still come up with great saleable ideas. Let's assume you've picked the section of a particular publication you want to write for, you've checked they take freelance ideas, and you're all set to pitch. Unless they're really desperate for a steady stream of run-of-the-mill ideas (and few are) you'll need to pitch something which covers a new, previously unidentified trend, or a new take on something which is happening already.

An example of the former might be some new legislation, a new travel destination or a new food trend. Awareness of the topic you're covering helps a lot here, which is why it's good to specialise in a select few areas. In the latter instance you might take an issue which has been covered extensively – so, for a parenting magazine, say, this could be the difficulty of parents finding childcare – and look at it differently. Perhaps you might address the issue of parents who choose to use their extended family to look after their children, or who take their babies into the office.

In order to get better at pitching, it helps to regularly read the publications you're aiming at. You'll also find you improve with every set of pitches you send. As topics change, you might find yourself updating old pitches and making them even better. So keeping a bank of pitches you've written will help you to practise and progress.

You should also know:

- Exactly who you are pitching by name.
- Whether they have any particular areas they need covering, and preferably times when it's most convenient to pitch them.
- Which section of the newspaper and magazine you're aiming at.
- The specific page or pages of the section where your ideas will fit – and that these sections take freelance work.

Focus, focus, focus

For most people, pitching is the fun part. Of course writing up a piece can be fun too. But nothing beats letting your mind wander over the possibilities of creative ideas for a new publication. Take your time. You'd be surprised how the calibre of your ideas improves over the course of a solid few hours.

As with your research on where to pitch, focus is key too. When you're coming up with ideas for a publication, you should be concentrating on ideas which are right for it, and it alone. If you have a great idea for something else, write it down and come back to it later.

It can be all too easy to get caught up in thinking about what you personally would like to cover. When you're thinking of ideas, it should be the readership that is foremost in your mind. If you're pitching to a trade magazine for restaurants, for example, the readership is most likely to be concerned with strategies that can make their establishment more money, and maximise their efficiency, rather than reviews of other establishments or the latest falling-out between famous head chefs.

Look at the themes of what has been covered already, and try to identify the motivation behind them. In some cases, of course, this motivation will be that a particular supplement has been engineered to attract advertising, so the content will have been geared to support this. But advertising is only part of what determines content. An editor will always keep their readers firmly in mind, and cover themes which they know people will want to read about in their publication.

REMEMBER: **Business and emotion don't mix.**

It's all very well to pitch something you're interested in, but when you're starting out it's best not to formulate ideas with a view to righting a personal grievance or exposing an issue which troubles you personally. The publication is the customer, not your soapbox.

Supporting material

Using the magazine itself, together with some other titles, can be a good way of brainstorming, and as you want your ideas to be outstanding it's worth taking the time here. Once you've started freelancing regularly, and cover a particular subject, you should build expertise which will make coming up with new ideas faster. But in the beginning put the hours into making your pitch count. Think laterally, but not too laterally. Could this idea really make it into this particular publication? Wishful thinking doesn't count.

Keeping abreast of the latest news is also helpful. And if you're pitching on 'serious' subjects like money and employment, latest changes in government policy and new legislation will provide you with invaluable inspiration for ideas. This kind of information is readily available on government and trade union websites, and is not an area which the average member of public takes a ready interest in. So if you can scan through the content of an upcoming change in the law, and find an angle which makes it interesting, you've got yourself a very saleable idea.

Compelling writing

In many cases, you will find that you can make even dull facts into strong stories. To give you an example of how this might work, let's take a news example and see how it can be transformed into a feature idea.

> *DfES Rolls Out New Modern Apprenticeships*
> *In a drive to improve apprenticeship opportunities the Department of Education and Skills has now launched two new modern apprenticeship programmes. Students interested in apprenticeships can now enrol in courses which cover 'office administration' and 'call centre administration'.*
>
> *"We're keen to see that apprenticeships reflect the contemporary jobs market," explains a spokesperson for the DfES. "And we think these new programmes offer increased opportunity for young people to gain employable skills and a recognised workplace qualification. They can also earn up to £70 a week whilst training."*

'How boring,' you might think. And an editor would agree with you. It might be the kind of 'news' which gets top billing on the education pages of a government website, or a few case studies in an education trade magazine if they're pushed for news. But it hardly deserves more than a few lines in a national newspaper.

But this is where your role as a freelance writer comes in. It's your job to make this interesting, because not only does it technically count as news in one of its purest forms, its boring nature will probably mean that most people have overlooked it.

So let's think about it in more detail. If we investigate a little further, we'll notice that apprentices are paid not a wage, but a nominal sum every week. This sum is less than they'd make full-time, but compensates the fact they are in a trainee position. This seems fair enough, as a trainee hairdresser is hardly worth the pay of a trained one – but the salary can, nevertheless, be considerably lower than the minimum wage. Is this strictly fair? Or even legal, on a government scheme?

Now we can see the beginnings of a story emerging. Because if you team the low salary with the expansion of the scheme, you'll realise that young people apprenticing as office workers and call-centre staff are also being paid less than the minimum wage.

I don't know about you, but I can think of numerous positions in offices and call centres which are available to untrained eighteen year olds for full pay. Not only that, such places are usually only too happy to take on staff in a junior role (it doesn't take long to become proficient with a photocopier), and call centres in particular usually provide comprehensive training whilst paying a full wage.

From a boring piece of legislation you now have the makings of quite an interesting story.

- Why should an office junior be paid less than the minimum wage for an NVQ which may or may not be as useful as four years' direct experience?

- Is a young person taking one day a week to train in 'office admin' getting the same kind of long-term career benefits as one who will become qualified in careers such as hairdressing, engineering, plumbing, or bricklaying, for example?

These are the kind of interesting questions which will see their way into a winning pitch. In fact, this particular story formed the basis of several commissions on the subject of young apprentices. So let's see how the end result of this news analysis might look:

The Unfortunate Apprentice
The government wants to encourage thousands more young people to work as apprentices. Pity they haven't thought to pay them, says Catherine Quinn.

It's a common employment debate – the UK is short of thousands of useful young people to take up apprenticeships. These NVQ-associated placements provide a vocational environment for young people to gain qualifications up to a degree equivalent. And as apprenticeships tend to fill skill gaps in the jobs market, the government is keen to boost numbers. A pity, then, that these placements are the only gainful employment in Britain where an office worker can legally be paid less than a call-centre operator in India.

- Over the last four years, the government has looked with increasing zeal to encourage young people into apprenticeships.
- Whilst these are frequently 'hands-on' vocations like engineering, an increasing number of millennial positions are admin based.
- Unfortunately, placements are the only UK work not covered by the minimum wage, and the TUC has examples of staff on as little as £1.53 an hour.
- For staff learning a complicated trade, employers might argue they are gaining from the experience, but for admin staff who could be paid full wages for the same position, the argument seems strained.
- Case studies of office apprentices and employers who take them on.

This article appeared in The Guardian, *12/2/2002.*

Finding the angle

How you come up with your own ideas is up to you. But in general your role is to take the often-dry subject of straight news, and give it an angle which would make a lot of people want to read it.

In terms of how you write it, obviously your pitch should read smoothly, and be free of typos and errors of grammar and spelling. But the other technique which comes under the remit of good writing is to structure an introduction which really pulls the reader in. Start dramatically, capture the imagination, and write in a way which makes whoever is reading it want to read on.

Here are two examples of the same idea for a seafood magazine on abalone (a shellfish). You might wonder how you could possibly make such an article interesting, but this is your skill as a freelancer. The first is written in a perfectly acceptable format for a pitch. But you can see how the second would probably be a more interesting option for an editor.

[HEADLINE]

All That Glistens

[STANDFIRST]

As a seafood delicacy to rival caviar and lobster, even the shell of abalone is a valuable commodity. Catherine Quinn finds out why this revered shellfish is selling out fast.

Pitch one
Fresh abalone, like beluga caviar, is big business on the black market. Known as paua in New Zealand, perlemoen in South Africa, and ormer in Guernsey, this seafood delicacy is extremely popular across Asia, Africa and the antipodes. And like caviar, the sheer demand for abalone has led to stocks being seriously depleted and illegal poaching.

Pitch two
The perimeter fences have been cut, and torches dimmed as the poachers prepare for the hunt. A successful trip can make them several hundred dollars in under an hour, provided they evade the African police. But rather than heavy rifles, these fugitives carry diving gear, and are searching for a more aquatic kind of white rhino.

Structuring your pitch

There are lots of different formats to pitch to editors. The most popular is the head-sell, shown in the examples used so far, which you can send with or without a headline and standfirst (the little bit of running commentary before your introduction).

Some writers just send a few bullet points for each idea to show what they'd cover, with a title to suggest what the article will be about. Others opt for a few sentences on each idea, and send long lists – mimicking the style of editorial brainstorming meetings where writers bandy around countless ideas before settling on a handful. Another classic style is the 'pitch letter', where the idea is sold through a written discussion of how the writer hit upon it, and why they think it would be perfect for the specific magazine in question. The latter involves a bit of extra work every time you pitch because it has to be tailored to each magazine, whilst the head-sell can be more easily rejigged a bit and sent out to lots of different places. But many writers have a lot of success with this format. It all comes down to what you feel you would do best, and a bit of experimentation.

The moral of the story is that there's no 'right' way to pitch. The best pitches are ones which win work, and these can take many forms. With enough practice, you'll hit on the pitch style that works best for you.

How do different pitches work?

The thing which most tends to interest new writers is what a successful pitch actually looks like. Obviously, now you've seen a few 'head-sell' pitches, you should have an idea of a format which works. As I mentioned earlier, however, everybody is an individual, and pitch formats vary considerably.

Learning the hard way: the head-sell

I've experimented with several styles of pitch, and the one which works best for me is the head-sell. I like this approach for a number of reasons. Firstly, it crams quite a lot of information into a very readable amount of text, so an editor glancing over your ideas won't see reams of writing which they have to get through. When you consider that many writers pitch an entire A4 page letter covering the merits of just one idea, whilst you can fit about three head-sells on a page, I think this is a real advantage.

The second major benefit is it immediately allows an editor to imagine that particular idea as it would run in their

---

> *publication. There's no need for them to think how it might start, or why it might be readable. The introduction is all there for them as it would be in print.*
>
> *Head-sells also use the existing advantages of publication format, in the short forms of a headline and then a standfirst to very quickly give an editor an idea of what they're reading. So by the time they've even got to the opening text they should have a fair idea of what will be covered.*
>
> *Last but not least, it calls upon your précis skill as a writer, which is a useful thing to showcase. Believe it or not, a big problem for many editors is cutting down extra text in features submitted by overzealous freelancers.*

As you can probably guess, I'm advising that you send your first pitches in this format, as I think it will give you the best chance of them being noticed. But if you're really stuck on another method, then feel free to experiment. Other written forms which work for me and other writers include:

The bulleted list

Like a shortened version of the head-sell. This form uses only around four or five bullet points to detail the content of the piece, and maybe an explanatory headline.

Australian Vegetarian Restaurants
- Despite the national predilection for meat pies and roo steaks, vegetarianism accounts for a generous portion of the antipodean food trade.
- The first (now legendary) vegetarian restaurant Shakahari opened in Melbourne in the 1970s, and since then highly-rated restaurants have followed suit all over Australia and New Zealand.
- Top Ten – the best rated vege haunts from Sydney to Tasmania.
- Surprising finds – some outback vegetarian classics.
- Comments and expertise from the Australian Vegetarian Society.

Advantages
- Quick to write.
- Quick for an editor to read.
- Allows several ideas to be sent in one go.

Disadvantages
- Might not be enough information to convince an editor to commission.
- Lacks a compelling introduction.
- Limits your ability to showcase your writing.

The pitch letter

This is often more like a full mini-CV, as it usually covers not only the idea but also a bit about the writer in general and why they're qualified to write it. It often also goes into detail about why the idea would appeal to the readership, so it's appealing to different aspects of the editorial need to pitch.

This approach works really well for many writers, and might be a good choice if you have an idea which you personally are particularly qualified to write for some reason. The downside is that it's not so suited for the first-timer, because the length naturally lends itself to including clips, or excessive personal biography which you may not have in enough detail to impress.

Dear Editor,

As a freelance writer with a keen interest in *Mother and Birth Magazine*, I am approaching you with a possible story idea.

I've noticed that your publication hasn't covered the subject of twins for some time, despite the fact this accounts for one in ten births and is a figure rising considerably due to the advent of artificial insemination.

As a twin myself I'd like to suggest an article which addresses parenting twins, and how to approach issues such as dressing them in the same clothes and allowing them individual identities. There are many opinions on the subject, from those who think denying their children's 'twinness' is selfishness on the part of the parents, to mothers and fathers of twins who insist on celebrating their originality.

I would propose to address this topic from the first-person perspective as a twin, and use a number of case studies to illustrate the different views. I would also be speaking with TAMBRA – the Twins and Multiple Births Association – on their views on the subject.

To give you a little more information on me, I'm a freelance writer with considerable experience of writing on pregnancy, birth, and childcare issues. I contribute regularly to *Pregnancy and Birth* and *Junior*, as well as a number of other publications.

If you'd like to find out about this idea in more detail, please do get in touch.

Advantages
- Provides comprehensive detail of an idea.
- Allows for an explanation of why you are the best person to write it.
- Gives more scope to reassure an editor that you're pitching them individually, rather than sending out blanket submissions.

Disadvantages
- Is lengthy and time-consuming to produce.
- Length means it has more margin for simple errors.
- Only allows one idea to be sent at a time.

The headed list
Rather than just one, two, or three ideas, this format goes for sheer quantity, listing a number of short ideas as a sentence each. Personally, I think this is a bit too much of a scattergun approach. But if you're pushed for time and have been asked to brainstorm a number of ideas, it could be a good strategy. This might be an example for a women's magazine:

- Interview with Courtney Love – love her or loathe her, she's seen by many as an icon.
- Getting fit in trapeze class – a new trend on the London celebrity circuit.
- Is he Mr Right? Experts comment on how to tell if the man you're dating is fill-in or marriage material.

Advantages
- Allows many different ideas to be sent in one go.
- Reassures an editor that you can formulate many good ideas.
- Is quick to write and send.

Disadvantages
- May suggest to an editor that your approach is "I'll write anything!" rather than a considered appraisal of a feature which would work in their publications.
- May overwhelm an editor with too many ideas at once.
- Lacks the detail to reassure an editor that you can deliver on the ideas suggested.

The right way to pitch

As you can see from the varieties above, editors don't scan potential ideas looking for a 'correct' format which proves a writer is professional. Pitches come in all shapes and sizes, and the best ones communicate a good idea as quickly as possible.

You may find that an approach which works for one person doesn't for another, and so on and so forth. This is simply to do with the incredible variety which is the human race, so don't worry too much about sticking to a particular format, or that your approach is 'wrong'. The chances are even the editor doesn't know the 'correct' way to send a pitch, so who knows, you could even be educating them.

A word from the editors

"Personally, I get swamped with emails and this is not always the best way to make first contact, because you're bunching yourself in with all the PR guff, random queries and spam. I prefer a – short

– introductory phone call, followed up by an email with strong feature ideas."

"Think about timing. If you make contact on a press day when people are under pressure, at best you're going to get overlooked, at worst you're going to piss someone off. Look up the publication date and get in touch the day before, when most magazines will have gone to press."

Andrew Williams, Deputy Editor, William Reed Business Publications

Don't get hung up on one idea

Whichever format you find works for you, don't get too concerned about one idea in particular. You'll be surprised how often an editor bypasses your dynamite un-pass-up-able idea in favour of one which you personally weren't so sold on. It could be that the editor has run something similar already, that they have some subjective prejudice against it, that you haven't pitched as well as you might have done, or simply that it's not as good an idea as you thought. So don't get hung up on getting one single idea in print.

Often when you do that, editors somehow consistently miss the genius of it. Of course, sometimes you have an idea which you just 'know' is great for a particular editor, and you're right. I've certainly had a few of these – and I've also had ideas consistently turned down which were in my opinion of undeniable brilliance. I suppose they weren't that great after all. Placing all your emphasis on one idea can also have the effect of blinding you to the low-freelance take-up of a particular section, because it might be suitable for only a few categories.

Learning the hard way: getting hung up on an idea
I once pitched an idea to the women's pages on The Guardian, *on hostessing in Japan. The hostess trade is like a modern-day geisha phenomenon, where girls work in bars making flirty chit-chat with men, pouring their drinks and so on. It's commonly mistaken as prostitution in the west, but it's actually a fascinating insight into Japanese culture.*

At the time, the World Cup was being held in Japan (it was a while ago) and I had actually worked as a hostess in a hostess club in Tokyo a few months previously. As far as I was concerned this was the idea that was going get me onto those

---

women's issues pages. Here was an actual real-life hostess, who already freelanced, offering her first-hand account of a controversial industry during a time when Japan features were in big demand.

Surely it would be simply impossible for an editor of the women's pages to turn down such an idea?

Well, sadly it wasn't impossible, and my story never got published. The editor did express a real interest, but after five or so chase-ups spanning a year and several changes of editor I realised it was time to give up. Looking back, it wasn't the idea that was the problem. It was the fact that I was so convinced this was a saleable piece I had ignored the golden rules of whether an editor is open to pitches.

The facts of the matter were that the women's page was a single page, covering a single feature which was run only fortnightly, and had an entire editor all to itself to staff it. The editor herself even told me this when I phoned her to chase, but I was so blinded by my great idea that I ignored one of the most important rules of freelancing – if there's no space for your idea, you're wasting your time selling it.

It's an easy mistake to make. We all have great ideas, and it can be very hard to let them go once you've written them up as pitches. But this is one of the lessons that you learn as a freelancer. You'll have many, many great ideas when you're pitching at a professional level, and not all of them will get into print. If you're lucky you can come back to them in a year or so, rewrite them a bit, and suddenly they'll sell. But it's important to keep with the process of pitching, rather than holding tight to one idea which you're convinced is more newsworthy than the rest. It's sad when editors don't recognise the potential of pitches which you know could be great features, but equally, they often know something you don't. And besides, they're the customer so you have to bow to their superior knowledge in any case.

Sending out your pitches

Three is the magic number

So how many pitches should be you sending out? I could give you a 'how long is a piece of string?' style answer on this, but you'll be pleased to know that in my opinion at least there is a definite here.

The optimum number is **three**. This is just the right amount to give an editor the impression that you can consistently come up with great ideas, and few enough that they don't feel a shudder of over-worked dread when they look at how long your email or letter is. The key is to get as much material to an editor as you can, whilst simultaneously giving them the impression that it will only take a few minutes to consider your proposals. Three is the perfect amount.

All three ideas have to be really good though – that's the point of sending more than one. So resist the temptation to pad out your one great idea with a couple of generic pitches. The reason why this approach works is because your batch of ideas is working as your entire recommendation.

In a way your pitches are doing the job of an interview for you, mapping out your talents more concisely and clearly than a good CV. And remember, you're selling your talent as much as your ideas with the first few pitches. If you've got one great idea and a few not-so-good ones, you undermine the whole package and even run the risk of casting doubt on your ability to write the good one, because it could be a fluke.

Your motivation is to convince an editor that you're a great potential freelancer, so that even if they pass on the first batch of ideas you send they'll have a thought in their head that you're good, and will be more eager to see future pitches from you.

How to send them

When you've got your three brilliant ideas, it's really up to you how to send them over. But I would recommend for the most part that you ask the editor how they would like to receive your ideas.

Snail mail

A tiny handful of editors prefer to receive pitches in hard copy as letters. These editors are usually older and often just prefer a document they can hold in their hand out of habit.

Before you silently complain about the extra effort spent printing and posting, you should realise that this preference can be a real advantage for freelancers. After all, in the age of information, how many freelancers are going to bother sending a letter rather than an email? So if you find an editor who wants pitches sent as letters, then indulge them. You'll be one of the few who do, and your ideas will get preferential treatment for your efforts.

In my experience, the few editors who like letters *always* commission or express interest in my ideas when I send them this way. How's that for good returns? And all for only a little extra effort of printing off some ideas and mailing them. If only more editors had this little whim for me to capitalise on, but there are very few left. Incidentally it's also a sign of a self-confident editor if they're happy to expect things a certain way, and that's a good thing.

Learning the hard way: keep an open mind

I once worked for an editor who actually refused to take calls made on a mobile phone as the reception wasn't as clear, and insisted on being called only by landline. This makes him sound like a difficult man, but in fact he was simply old enough not to feel self-conscious about working in a particular way (I also suspect it was difficult for him to hear on a crackling mobile connection). He was a really great editor to work with, and I enjoyed his confident manner hugely.

I soon learned that preferences like these are not necessarily the mark of an editor who is difficult to please, and accommodating them can put your ideas at the top of the pile.

Email

For the most part, however, editors will ask you to send ideas by email. This is easier as you can send out lots at once using cut and paste, and you also have a handy archive system if you need to check back to see what you've sent.

A word to the wise with emails, however. Editors everywhere have the same enormous dislike of being mass-mailed. It happens to them every day with writers and PRs, and with varying degrees of inaccuracy on the part of the sender, so you can imagine how tiresome it gets.

By all means do a bit of cutting and pasting to save yourself time, but never let it *look* as though you're cutting and pasting. *Check, recheck and check again* that some embarrassing cross-over hasn't happened and you've addressed them by another editor's name or mentioned a rival publication.

The same goes for any pitches you're mailing out. You should always tailor each and every pitch to a particular publication anyway, but if you have two which are *really* similar, be sure you haven't included some tell-tale detail in the text that the ideas are going out to more than one person. The editor should always think an email is for them and them alone (even if that's not quite the case).

Pitch to the right person

Of course you'll already have made a few calls to find out who to send ideas to, and you should be mailing that person directly. If in doubt, pitch to the editor, who will always have the final say in whether your idea goes in their publication in any case. Certain publications are big enough to have a kind of hierarchy in place which gets sniffy about having 'just anyone' contact the editor, and will have deputies or other staff to field your call and make it difficult to get the right name.

In this instance I would be wary of spending too much time pitching and chasing. Magazines with editors who refuse to take phone calls from freelancers are rarely in the market for much material, as it means they've got enough staff to allow the editor to become rather delusional about their self-importance.

> **Web tip:**
> If you're not sure the 'head-sell' layout is for you, take a look at a number of different pitch formats and styles at
> www.nocontactsnoproblem/pitchexamples.html

Action plan

Ready... set... pitch! You're now ready to start pitching, so formulate your killer ideas using the tips in this chapter, and send them out to the right person in the format they've requested.

1. You'll already have some ideas written for your most intimidating publications, so now it's time to write for those which sounded like good leads.

2. Use the standard you've already set for yourself in formulating pitches for the more difficult editors, and ensure you're matching that same high standard.

3. In total, you should aim to have written three pitches for ten different editors – so thirty in total, although these can overlap if you're pitching to similar titles.

4. Send your pitches out in whichever format the editor has stated a preference for.

5. Good luck!

6

Help! I don't have any clips

The fear of most new writers is that an editor will demand they supply a portfolio of high-calibre clips, to prove they've previously been published extensively. In this chapter we'll discover not only why this isn't always necessary, but also how to come up with solutions to this potential problem.

In this chapter, you'll:

- Find out what to do when an editor asks you for clips.
- Learn some first-timer short-cuts to get clips of your work.
- Discover how to use celebrity interviews to get clips.
- Learn how to get face-to-face meetings with editors.

Clips – the Catch 22 of the first-timer

If you've read up to this point, you may have been thinking the entire time, "Well, fine in theory, but what about when an editor asks me for clips?" Or maybe you have no idea what a 'clip' is, but have a vague feeling that an editor would want to see evidence of your writing abilities before commissioning you.

So here's the classic Catch 22 for first-timers. You can't get a commission without clips, and you can't get clips without a commission. When you haven't written for an editor before, it's standard practice for them to ask to see some of your writing which has previously been published. The problem is that as a first-time writer you won't have any clips to show, so you have no place to start and no place to go. This dilemma prevents a lot of would-be freelancers from getting going from a standing start.

The traditional route to getting clips

The standard industry practice is to work your way up into writing features in this order:

1. Do your time first as a work experience, maybe collecting some small clips.

2. Then perhaps as an assistant of some kind, writing filler pieces.

3. After several years, if you work hard and build up good expertise, you'll be rewarded with a promotion to sub-editor.

4. If you avoid getting typecast as a sub-editor for the rest of your career, and you've demonstrated enough talent, you'll get a role where you can write features – either as deputy editor, features editor, staff writer or similar.

Sounds like a lot of work, doesn't it, when you can write features already?

Luckily the 'No Contacts' method will see you in print much faster than this. As you can see from this traditional career path, you are not really in a position to be showing your clips as a professional freelancer until you've reached the editorial part of a conventional staffing structure.

Even at this point, in fact, years of experience on a handful of publications can tend to create a rather narrow range of clips, which may be unhelpful. After all, if you're pitching an employment editor who asks to see your writing, and you can only show them clips from food trade magazines, you're making it pretty obvious that your writing ability is not in their area, and the clips you have to show are limited.

Don't start small

So what can you do about this terrible circumstance? You'll be pleased to know that it's not as bad as it first seems.

Learning the hard way: building a portfolio of clips
When I first started writing I placed an awful lot of store by clips. I dutifully cut out anything and everything which had ever been published with my name on it (and some without) and squirreled them away as evidence for editors that I was

indeed a published writer. The more I had, the better. I even set them out in a big artist's portfolio, confident that the day would come when I would lug this thing along to the offices of a potential employer and talk them through my wealth of experience in print.

Track forward seven years or so and I'm on a press trip with a fellow writer who has been in the trade for a decade at least. We are enjoying a good joke about how we both used to save all our clips – "I think I even had an artist's portfolio with them all laid out!" he confesses to our mutual mirth.

Nowadays we hardly ever show clips to editors, and we certainly wouldn't wheel along an entire portfolio to a meeting of any kind. We just assume as we're published already that an editor won't need to bother with clips.

For the seasoned freelancer, clips build up very quickly so that after even only a few years, writers are very unlikely to try and get copies of all of them. I occasionally cut out big ones I really like and keep them loosely slung in a box file, but I don't have every single piece of work stored away neatly.

Because I'm already published many times, I don't feel the need to inundate an editor with hundreds of clips – I assume they'll realise I have them all in store and it's too much effort to tediously scan, email or post them. Unsurprisingly, as experienced freelance writers have this attitude, a lot of editors do too, and you'll find they often care far less than you might imagine about seeing concrete evidence of your writing.

Naturally as a first-timer you will want examples of your work in print – that's why you're reading this book, after all – so I've some even better news for you. There is a way for you to build clips which will impress any editor almost immediately. *The secret is to start at the top.* Rather than wasting your time toiling for the trade press, working through to consumer titles and building small filler clips and odd trade features, go straight to the top titles that you want to be published in. Or more specifically, head for the national newspaper press.

Big editors don't ask for clips

In my experience as a freelance writer, a reasonable number of magazine editors ask to see clips – or at least mention in passing that they'd like to see some. Interestingly, these editors most often work on trade magazine titles, which would suggest that they are either less confident than their consumer magazine colleagues, or that they suffer the effects of bad writing from freelancers more frequently. Either way, it's a trend worth noting. (Although to be fair, trade magazines will probably be more forgiving of less prestigious clips, provided they're well written.)

But here's a more important actuality. In my entire freelance career, which now spans eight years and counting, I've written hundreds of articles for national newspapers in the UK, including *The Guardian*, *The Times*, *The Telegraph*, *The Independent* and *The Mirror*. And do you know how many editors from those titles have asked to see clips? *None. Zero. Not one.*

Not a single editor on a newspaper has ever asked to see examples of my work. I can't tell you why this is. I think it's a combination of confident editors who assume that a well-pitched idea means a good writer (which it does), and a high-pressure environment with a fast turn-around. They don't have time to trawl through a writer's clips, and if a writer's work is no good, then they'll either send it back to be rewritten or just not use you again. After all, there's plenty of other good writers pitching them, because they're on the nationals after all.

So there you go – the secret to tapping into a market of editors who probably won't ask you for clips. And once you have a feature-length article written in a national newspaper, it goes a long way to confirming your status as a professional freelancer to other editors. After all, what editor wouldn't assume you to be a good writer if you can say confidently that you write for *The Guardian*? Which is true, even if you've only written one feature.

What to do when an editor asks you for clips

I can't emphasise enough here how it is confidence more than ability which will get you that first vital commission. If you phone the editor of a publication sounding like a confident professional, they will often have no reason to question that this is what you really are.

REMEMBER: An editor doesn't want to spend time checking a writer's work and credentials.

They've got better things to do. They'd prefer to have a writer ready to use with no bother, and this is particularly true of national newspapers.

What you may be worrying about now, however, is if the worse-case scenario happens and an editor does ask you for clips, and you're placed in the embarrassing position of having to explain that you've picked up the phone, described yourself as a freelance writer, and here you are with no evidence to back you up.

Whilst I wouldn't ever advocate outright lying about your experience, I don't think there's anything wrong in hedging a bit in order to secure yourself a commission which you know you're perfectly capable of fulfilling. So if an editor does ask you, don't make a big deal of it. Don't act like you've been put on the spot. Often, if an editor does ask, they'll throw it into a conversation casually – usually after you've talked with them for a while establishing whether they have work or not – and they'll say something like "Oh, and do you have any examples of your work you can send over?" If this happens:

1. Adopt the same casual tone.
2. Agree that of course you have some examples (what professional freelancer wouldn't?).
3. Say you'll send over some clips.

What have I got you into? Now you're now placed in the position of promising something you can't deliver. You'll have to either come up with some clips reasonably fast, or hope they'll forget they asked in the first place.

In fact the latter circumstance happens more often than you might assume. I suspect that most editors who ask for clips only do so out of a vague sense that this is the proper thing to do, and are not really bothered about reading anything. If you've sold an editor on an idea, I would say you've almost certainly convinced them of your professionalism already.

Remember too that clips are only a small part of the picture, and keep them in perspective. Editors may claim to set a lot of store by them, but without realising it they will usually be far more sold on your professional manner and your great ideas.

REMEMBER: **As a freelance writer, sending great examples of your work will almost never get you commissions, but sending good pitches will.**

Undoubtedly, a few editors who have been burned by bad writing will want to check out your style thoroughly. If you've managed to secure a commission from a national, then you are in the happy position of being able to name-drop this into the conversation. And editors are usually impressed enough by these big-name titles to leave it at that.

Getting around the issue of clips

If you're pretty sure they won't commission you until they've seen evidence of your work, then don't panic. Remember – all they've asked for is an example of your writing. *It doesn't necessarily have to be as a published clip.*

It's perfectly acceptable to have something on a Word file. Even full-time freelancers like myself don't have too much time to constantly scan articles and make them up as PDFs so that an editor can see a piece in all its published glory. They're often harder to read in this style anyway, so you're entirely legitimate sending your work like this.

So your next steps are to:

4. Write something good.
5. Make sure it's *really* good.
6. Send it over as a Word document.

They're asking to see your writing, after all, not the skills of which-ever designer laid it out. If you're wondering what I mean by 'send something good', you'll have to make your own judgement. But seeing as how you're writing something with one particular editor in mind, it makes sense to take advantage of a golden opportunity to present them with something highly similar to what they already publish.

Don't skimp on the quality either. Yes, this means more work for you, and unpaid work at that (although who knows, you might be able to pitch and sell the piece later down the line). But what's a few days' extra work compared to several years toiling as a junior on a trade title for a few measly clips? You can of course be creative if you're using quotes and facts in your masterpiece – this is never going to be subject to the rigours of fact-checkers on a publication and is written purely to showcase your writing style.

Write your piece as something which may have been published in a competitor's publication. The key here is tactical omission rather than trying to excuse your lack of experience. Don't say too much about the work and where it came from. Instead, steer the situation back to the most important aspect, which is whether they like your ideas enough to commission you to write an article for them. Incidentally, this is exactly how a writer with years of experience would behave. Who has time to give their life story to every single editor when you've had hundreds of articles in print already?

Warning – examples you should never send

If you have a few small clips already, a word of warning. There are times when a poor choice of published clip will do less for you than a well-written piece presented as a Word document. In fact there are some things you shouldn't send under any circumstances.

If you're using the 'No Contacts' method, never, ever, under any circumstances send:

- Articles you wrote for a student newspaper (with the publication title evident).
- 'Filler' (or very small) pieces you've written on work experience or in a similar capacity.
- Any writing which doesn't have the appearance of being written for a national publication.
- Any writing you did for any other purpose than professional feature writing, which includes work newsletters, press releases and company brochures.

By offering to send any of this kind of writing, you're actually making yourself look far less experienced than if you simply hedge a bit and agree to send something over.

Think about it. Would you commission someone with patently no experience at all to write a piece for a national publication? Of course you wouldn't. If you were feeling kind you might suggest that they send something in 'on spec' (a term we'll come to later). But really, that would be creating extra work for yourself, as you couldn't allocate it a slot until you'd read it through and checked the quality – not great for a busy editor when the whole purpose of a freelancer is to save you time.

The same goes for filler pieces you may happen to have built up in a work experience or some other staff capacity. Even if you've got a ton of them, a small collection of tiny filler pieces will show a potential commissioning editor that you're in a junior position with not much experience.

This will have the likely effect of making them suspect your abilities, or worse, treating you with the condescension of an indulgent mentor helping a fledging writer get into print. "That doesn't sound so bad," you might think, but the aim here is to be a professional writer as soon as possible, not a charity project for an editor who thinks they're helping out a newcomer.

The latter circumstance may get you some good advice, and it may even get you a work experience or (at a real push) a junior staff position. But what it won't do is get your writing recognised and published as the work of a professional. So when you're talking to an editor about your clips, talk about professional feature-length ones only please, or don't mention them at all.

The (almost whole) truth and nothing but the truth

This said, you should never, ever tell outright lies about your experience. Whilst tactical omission might lend a certain impression of your experience, it's very different from telling an untruth. So unless you've written something or been commissioned for a particular publication, don't say you have.

This is especially true of magazines, which are quite incestuous places where everybody knows everybody else and which frequently switch around staff roles on the same titles. The big magazine houses often have staff from different titles working right next to each other. So you certainly wouldn't want to be in the position where an editor leans over to a colleague and asks them if you've written for them, only to be met with a blank stare and an avowal that they have never spoken to you.

It's one thing not to blunder in with wide admissions of your inexperience, but it's quite another to put yourself at risk of being found out as someone who lies about their work as a freelancer. Not only would that be incredibly embarrassing, but it would also get you remembered amongst editors for all the wrong reasons.

By all means don't rush to tell an editor that you've never been published before. But don't start getting too creative with your experience either.

A word from the editors

"If you've got a few clips, either from student publications or small pieces from work experience, send only three across without any further explanation. You're giving the impression to the editor that 'there's more where that came from'.

And if you have no clips at all, pitching an idea which only you can write can get you a commission."

Barbara Rowlands, Journalist and Programme Director
of Journalism, City College

"Who do you write for?"

This is the last thing that a new writer wants to hear, but rest assured, editors very rarely ask the question. And funnily enough, when it does come up, it's often because an editor wants to check that you *don't* write for a particular rival publication, rather than that your name is splashed across the by-lines of every major daily paper.

Certain consumer (and very rarely trade) publications get a little high-handed about decreeing that a freelancer with a specialism in their area should write for them and them alone. Quite how they imagine a freelancer could make a living writing solely for their publication is beyond me, but it's as well for you to know that the motivation for this kind of enquiry often stems from this concern, rather than from a suspicion that you are under-experienced. Sometimes, of course, editors do simply want to check you've been published somewhere half decent, and will ask accordingly.

So what can you do in this terrible situation? Unfortunately, you'll probably have to come clean and admit that you're just starting out. This may well prejudice the editor against any ideas you then send to them (although it may not), but it's a price you'll have to pay for honesty.

How to get real clips

The other solution to the problem is to get yourself some real clips to send over. After all, it's all very well knowing that editors won't mind a Word document, but when you're starting out *you'll* probably feel better about sending over clips which have obviously made it into print. The good news is that getting clips which are good examples of your work is not too difficult. The bad news is that is does tend to take a while for publications to chug through the print run, so you could be waiting a while for your precious clips after you've written them.

Student publications

If you're still a student, or are linked to a university or college in some capacity, then this can be a great way to get a large, feature-length article in print. To save yourself a bit of time, look for the less popular areas. So I wouldn't bother too much with pitching music features, for example, because this section is likely to be bursting at the seams with wannabe music journos.

You may be thinking at this point that I have specifically said not to send student clips, so why am I now advising you that this is a way to gain examples of your work? Well, whilst it's certainly true that I wouldn't have you advertising yourself as someone who writes for student publications, you don't have to say where a particular clip comes from. Just cut off the student title at the top of your page, and try to give the impression that it's from a bona fide national. Again, the key is tactical omission. If it's a piece which is obviously professionally written and laid out in a tolerably well-designed fashion, there is every chance that an editor will accept it as reasonable evidence that you can write to a good standard.

Advantages of student newspapers and magazines

- They're usually informal operations and are reasonably easy to get involved in.
- Print runs are often fast. So you could see an article you've written appearing in print in a matter of weeks.
- Publication quality is often fair, and clips can pass as from a local newspaper or similar.

Disadvantages of student newspapers and magazines

- They can be quite competitive, depending on which university or college is involved.
- Copy is not subject to the usual scrutiny of a professional publication and may appear with disastrous errors like typos.
- Your work won't be subject to extensive sub-editing, and may even be strangely reworded by an over-eager student journalist.

You certainly need to make sure your work is absolutely word perfect before you submit it – the last thing you need is a printed version of your work with obvious errors.

In the case of your words being badly altered, there's not too much you can do about it other than hope for the best. It doesn't often happen, but I've had the very first sentence of an article I submitted to a free publication reworded in a very odd way which only people of a certain age would have understood.

Other free publications

No access to a student publication? Don't worry. There are plenty of other publications out there that are easy to get into by merit of not paying any money. What's more, many of them give every impression of being the kind of newspaper or magazine with a proper freelance budget, and an editor is hardly likely to ask whether you got paid for a piece.

Seeking out publications which don't pay for freelance work is not too hard – just look for places that you know don't have too much money. Charities are a good place to start (although note that *The Big Issue* does pay freelancers), as many have a publication of some kind which they will be delighted to let you write in.

Trade unions and the left-wing press are another goldmine of unpaid opportunities to get into print in a professional-looking context. They tend to be very 'newsy' as well, which adds kudos to your clips. Most editors accept that someone with a strong news background can move across to softer subjects like food, but few consider it possible the other way around without strong evidence.

Another possibility is magazines and newspapers aimed at students. These are different from actual student publications in that they are professionally produced by corporate publishing houses. But many of them run to very meagre budgets, and given their target audience often use students to write their content gratis. Personally I think there are some moral issues here, as these publications are turning a profit so really should be paying their writers. Nevertheless they do offer a good chance to gain professional-looking clips (although covering student topics can tend to mark you out as a student yourself), and most editors will have no idea you've not been paid.

Local listings-style magazines also offer some opportunity to get work in print, but they're often focused on reviews and filler pieces, which are a bit small for your purposes. But if you have a local magazine which runs full-length feature pieces on the local area, for example, then they might be a good option to approach.

Not only are most of these places delighted to accept your ideas, they'll also be very understanding of the fact that you don't have any experience and often provide large, attractively laid-out clips. After all, they're not offering you any money, so they can hardly be sniffy about the calibre of writers who approach them. These publications do tend to take a little longer to roll around with the print run. But with any luck they can represent a real opportunity for you to build clips.

Celebrity short-cuts

Another little-known way to get a dynamite clip is to conduct celebrity interviews. These are a great deal easier to obtain than you might think, and they have a dual bonus of virtually guaranteeing you a commission whilst considerably enhancing the status of your finished clipping. After all, few student publications would turn down a celebrity interview, even if the person wasn't that famous, and the same goes for publications which get their content for free.

Getting hold of a celebrity

Making contact with a celebrity is very difficult, but tracking down and getting in touch with their agent is very easy. Agents are in the business of making bookings for their clients and a large part of their job is dealing with press and publicity. You can get contact details through whatever form of media the celebrity is most prominent in. So if they've written a book, phone their publisher; if they're on TV, phone the BBC; and if they're in music, phone their record label.

With the exception of the BBC, which can make it difficult to get hold of the right people, you'd be surprised how willing people are to hand over an agent's details. You're not asking for the celebrity's personal address, but rather you're taking the recognised route to offering them publicity, which is an entirely symbiotic process. Most agents are very nice too, and as accommodating as possible when it comes to fitting in interviews.

Keep it C-list

Don't go too famous, though. If you start targeting Hollywood superstars you're going to find it almost impossible to arrange an interview, even if getting hold of their agent is straightforward. Set your sights firmly 'C-list' at people who will be readily available. We're talking novelists (apart from the likes of JK Rowling), soap stars, singers in bands with several members, and people who have won well-known prizes like the Turner prize a couple of years back. These are all great fodder for interviews, as their names are usually in the public arena, but they're not necessarily busy every minute of the day and are probably only too willing to help oil the wheels of their own publicity machine.

Good signs to look for in a potential celebrity interview are:

- The celebrity has been out of the public eye for some time, but it now looks like they're courting publicity again.
- They've just got a new role in a musical or a theatre production (not TV or film).

- They've recently released a book or product (not a music album or release).

These celebs are normally actively seeking to gain press interviews, and as an added bonus you can often negotiate a few free copies of their book or product, or tickets to their production as a giveaway for whatever publication you're pitching to. This can make the interview more attractive to editors.

Accommodating the celebrity schedule

The thing which most celebrities are very short of is time, which is why I wouldn't recommend going after mega-celebs. It's not that they're not open to press interviews – in fact, a large part of their careers is formulated around their willingness to court publicity – but they simply don't have the time. A touring celebrity, for example, will often have not just every hour, but every last minute of their time scheduled to accommodate a gruelling regime of performances, interviews, signings, launches and so forth. So even though their agent may be keen to cram in extra, it is often simply impossible.

When it comes to contacting the lesser-knowns, you should be explaining to their agent that:

- You want a five- to ten-minute phone interview, rather than a face-to-face discussion. This gives you the best chance of getting hold of them, as you're really asking for very little of their time.
- You're writing (or pitching) the piece for a number of publications, in order to give the impression you are maximising the celebrity's time.
- You're keen to mention their product, book, production or whatever as part of the interview.

You don't have to say that you're still in the process of pitching publications. The chances of gaining the interview are probably around 50:50 at best, so play these odds to your advantage and go in with the best possible sell. In all honesty, if you get the interview but the article never appears in print, it is highly unlikely the agent will even notice. Press is a fickle business, and by no means one hundred percent of commissioned pieces make the newsstands.

You should also be aware that whilst the process of getting a celebrity interview is reasonably straightforward and accessible, the actuality of nailing down a busy celebrity amongst all the other things they're doing is more difficult. The solution to this is to play the numbers game, and contact several at once. Don't worry about over-stretching yourself – you can always find a market for an interview if you get it, and you're compiling useful contact details and information at the same time.

Some celebrities are 'out of the country' when you contact their agent. This is often a polite way of saying the celebrity in question is sick of the pressure and taking a well-earned break from the limelight. In this instance you can always ask when they're back, and even if it's several months away, make a follow-up call.

If you contact enough celebrities, you will get a phone interview sooner or later. When you do, you should immediately start finding out whether the smaller sections mentioned earlier could be interested. This is because if they decide they are, you'll need to interview with their specific criteria in mind. Many have rigid set questions which need to be answered, and you certainly don't want to be calling the agent back half an hour later saying there's a question you forgot to ask.

Where to place celebrity interviews

Once you've secured your interview, you can also phone around the nationals to see if you can find somewhere to place it. Don't bother with the big celebrity feature slots, though – these are filled months in advance by writers with an inside track on the celeb circuit. But many publications have a regular slot where they feature a celebrity, and it can be someone who is only marginally famous.

Small supplements in newspapers or regular short celeb interviews in magazines are often good bets for placing your piece. An office supplement, for example, may have a small weekly interview where celebrities talk about their first job, or an education paper may have a section where celebs talk about their best teacher. These kinds of places will often have a hard job getting hold of someone famous on such a regular basis, and will normally be delighted if you phone them up with a opportunity to fill another week.

Using the web to showcase your work

The information age is very much on the side of freelance journalists. Not only is it easier than ever before to access valuable information for an article, it's also a great way to get work published and showcase your writing.

For writers starting out it's also an opportunity to build a website which will act as your CV and your portfolio, and with the magic of web design you can make an impressive site to help bypass your lack of experience. Believe me, a well-designed website goes a long way. Most writers don't even have one, and editors are usually really pleased if you can refer them to a single site with examples of your work, rather than emailing them huge PDF attachments or Word documents to scan through.

Of the writers who do have a website, a lot of them are obviously home-spun creations with a tendency to archive every piece they've ever written. So if you create an attractive, well-designed site showcasing a discrete number of pieces in an accessible way, you've put yourself above the competition in the pitching process.

This is easier said than done, of course. I personally spent a reasonable amount of time learning HTML, which is not everyone's idea of fun. If you don't have a predilection for coding web pages, then find a friend or a local designer who can put together a good site for a small fee. It's perfectly acceptable to only showcase a few examples of your work on the site, and you don't have to be too forthcoming about where they were published either, if you're still waiting to get into print. Instead you can rely on your site to house them in a way which advertises you as a professional writer.

Beyond writing – pitching in person

Another technique to have editors overlook your lack of experience is by establishing some rapport with them before you get started. This isn't the same as spending years in the trade, building up contacts. Instead we're going to look at some ways of approaching editors that will cement you in their mind as a dynamic professional, thus neatly bypassing their need to see extra credentials from you in the form of clips.

The phone pitch

Some people are telephone people and some people aren't. I've had editors who have commissioned me for years by email, without once having a conversation with them on the phone. Many other editors, however, would always call to discuss what an article might involve, because this is what they find most comfortable.

It's quite easy to identify an editor who likes to talk on the phone, because you'll be calling them to see if they're commissioning, and the ones that like telephone conversations will keep you talking.

If you're a phone person yourself then there are a lot of advantages to explaining your pitch over the phone rather than writing it out in full. Once you've had a few articles commissioned by the same editor, you can save yourself a lot of time if you're able to ring them with an idea in embryo and have them commission it without the trouble of writing it all out. In addition, you pick up a great deal more clues and educational tips when you're talking over the phone, as editors will give you more information in the tone of their voice than you'd get in an email.

How should you go about phone pitching? The key is to sound confident and professional, so stand tall and keep a smile on your face as you call. Unless they're on deadline, most editors will hear you out and let you know what they think of your idea. You might not get a commission on the first call – they may ask you to email them further information, or come back to them when they're ready to commission. But you'll be covering vital groundwork when it comes to getting your work in print.

Arranging a face-to-face meeting

Business research shows that you are more likely to make a sale of any kind face to face than you are over the phone. In fact the numbers show that the relationship is around one in twenty sales for cold calling (which is what you're doing when you pitch) versus one in five face to face. So where possible, a well-made face-to-face meeting represents a good chance of getting a commission for the first-time writer. A little caveat to this is if you are or look very young: in this case appearing in person can prejudice an editor against you, due to your perceived youth and inexperience. So if you fall into this category it might be better to stick to the phone and let the maturity of your voice speak for you.

The five-minute elevator pitch

This is the kind of pitch that you'll use if you happen to have a few minutes to chat with an editor – at a networking event, for example. It's a classic business term based on the idea of a keen young entrepreneur selling their idea to a time-pressed executive who they've managed to collar, perhaps in the spare few minutes that they're in the elevator on the way to their office.

As a freelancer this model should have a lot of resonance for you, as editors normally want face-to-face pitches to be succinct and to the point.

But, you may be asking, how do you go about getting this all-important face time? In case you were in any doubt, newspapers and magazines keep highly secure offices, and you're unlikely to be able to even access the elevators, let alone ride up and down in them talking to editors.

The best way to get one-on-one contact is to offer yourself up for work experience. This way you get into the inner sanctum in a legitimate way, and it's fair to say the publication rather owes you some meaningful contact with their staff if you're working for free.

Luckily, the days of corner offices are more or less over and most editors are approachable at open plan desks, so it doesn't matter if you're not working in their area, or even on the same floor. Use stealth; find out where the section you're interested in is based by any means possible. Then, go for a wander to where they're working, check they don't look incredibly busy and harassed, take a deep breath, walk up to them and explain very politely that you're working in the offices at the moment, and you wondered if they might have five minutes in the next week for a quick cup of coffee and a chat about some freelance ideas you had in mind.

Editors get asked out to lunch and coffee all the time, so the chances are that being asked by someone who obviously has a right to be in the building, to a spot actually on the premises, will be more appealing to them than most such invites.

There's no doubt it takes a bit of confidence to try out this method, but you'll be surprised how friendly and amenable most editors are to sparing five minutes or so for a potential freelancer.

Guerrilla methods of getting face-to-face contact

You can try the same technique on the internal phone system, or even – although it's a bit sneaky – if you're not actually working in the offices. Just pretend that you are, and it means you can meet them on their territory whenever they're free.

You'll have to give a convincing reason why they should come down to reception and get you through security, of course, but you could just explain that your dates have been changed. The big factor here is that you're arranging to meet them in very convenient circumstances, which makes it easier for the editor.

Ironically, however, even though you may be willing to go all out to make this meeting happen, the dual advantage here is that it also looks like the venue is convenient for you. Most editors on large publications will have experienced the odd 'mad' writer who chases them at networking events and endlessly emails them. You want to make it very clear that you're not one of these desperate individuals, but rather a professional with your own busy schedule who is nevertheless keen for a meeting to ensure that your pitching is the best it can be.

For preference, by the way, an editor is more likely to agree to a meeting if you've approached them at their desk. That's just the way people work. If you've managed to get work experience and are wondering how on earth this can help your career, then it's also a good way to make it worth your while.

Once you've got hold of an editor in this time-pressured situation it's obviously very important to make the most of the window. Editors of nationals are at the receiving end of lots of invites and requests for their time, so don't aim to take any more than ten to twenty minutes of it. You're also busy and important, remember, so you have things you'll be needing to get back to. Make sure you cover the price of the coffees too.

Making it work – fast

Once you've snared the meeting, here are a few pointers to making it go your way. You don't have a lot of time to convince the editor you're a pro, so good ways to get them onside fast include:

- Pointing out an article from their section or publication you really liked (preferably one which they wrote). This will convince them you're a regular reader, which every editor loves to hear.

- Alluding to their target market, and how your idea fills a niche which hasn't been covered for those readers. You might say something like, "I've noticed that the recent sex discrimination legislation hasn't been covered much in the press, and I think it's something which would really be of interest to your readers, as young professionals. Do you think it's something you might think about commissioning for the magazine?"

- Asking if there are any particular areas which they have diffi-culty covering, and making positive noises about how they relate to your own interests and expertise.

If you come across well in person, remember that even if they're not interested in ideas you pitch on the day, it gives you a good reason to contact them later with more ideas and remind them of your first meeting.

> **Web tip:**
> Panicking about being asked for clips? On the website we've compiled a list of titles which are a good bet for generating unpaid clips, as well as a regular list of publications looking for work experience students.
> www.nocontactsnoproblem.com/getclips.html

Action plan

Whilst this chapter has been about the reasons why you don't necessarily need clips, first-time writers usually feel more comfortable with a few published items to show. So using the methods we've covered, put the steps in place to get a few non-professional clips to elevate your status as a writer.

1. Arrange yourself some work experience, start tracking down celebrity agents, look into building yourself a website, and get working on a few practice features.

2. Keep up the hard work until you have some decent-looking 'practice' clips to augment your soon-to-be-growing pile of nationally published work.

7

Chase-ups – the most important part of your job

Anyone can pitch editors, but not everyone takes the time to chase up their efforts with professional efficiency. Learn this fundamental skill and you'll always be ahead of the competition.

In this chapter, you'll:

* Discover why editors might not have got back in touch.
* Understand the importance of chase-ups.
* Learn how to chase up your pitches professionally.
* Choose a chase-up system which works for you.

They haven't got in touch – they hate my ideas!

A lot of writers shy away from chase-ups. It's understandable really. Most of us are under-confident starting out, and assume, rightly or wrongly, that an editor hasn't got in touch because they weren't interested in our ideas. Or worse, were so appalled at the limited nature of our pitches that they haven't even bothered to send an email rejecting them.

But chase-ups not only form a key part of your pitching regime, they are often what separates a would-be freelancer to one who is constantly in print. The reason for this is that editors are busy people, and the fact they haven't got back to you absolutely does not mean they didn't like your ideas.

There are many possible reasons why an editor hasn't got back to you, and most of them have nothing to do with the calibre of what you've sent. Here are just a few.

They haven't received them

You wouldn't believe how often this happens. When you're communicating by email or post, things can go missing, get deleted, or go into spam folders by mistake. Plus, in busy periods some editors can get a bit trigger-happy with the deleting of non-urgent material (and who can blame them?).

The outcome of this is that your precious ideas aren't even with the editor, let alone in their rejection pile. I have lost count of the times I've made a tentative phone call expecting an editor to say they didn't like my ideas, only to discover they didn't receive them and are very enthusiastic about having them resent. Quite often, on resending ideas I have then been commissioned fairly rapidly.

They've put them in a big folder to go through when they get a minute

This also happens a reasonable amount. It is quite incredible how long an editor can sit on an idea without commissioning it. The average runs to months rather than weeks, but I've had ideas commissioned after a year or more of patient chase-up phone calls.

The moral of the story here is don't be too impatient and put all your eggs in one basket. For every slow-moving editor there are faster ones who'll give you rapid responses. Do believe them when they say they've got it on file, though, as I've never come across an editor who used this as a strategy to fob off writers. They'll tell you if your work is not right.

This said, if an editor says that your ideas are 'not quite right for now' but claim they'll keep them on file, take it as a sign to send some different ones.

They've moved on and a replacement is doing their job

The world of print media is a very fickle thing, and editors change roles with astonishing regularity. If you've had an idea sitting with a particular publication for several months, it's not unlikely that the editor has moved on without forwarding their ideas file. Even if your ideas have been forwarded, new editors are sometimes a little hesitant about commissioning ideas from writers they know nothing about. So you need to phone up, introduce yourself (again) and resend the ideas to the new editor.

Sometimes, when roles change a few times in quick succession, it may indicate a time of unrest at the publication. My record for circulating staff in the same role has been about five in as many months, as a new appointment was made, remade, and the magazine was sold and resold to two different publishing houses. But after all that movement I was finally commissioned by the editor at the end of the line, who became a very good customer.

They're waiting for your call

This happens too. An editor might like your ideas, and be quite keen to commission them, but are waiting for the final nudge from you. Some editors don't like email too much and would prefer to make arrangements by telephone, and others procrastinate when it comes to commissioning new writers, and a timely phone call is all that is needed to nudge them into action.

They didn't like your ideas and didn't bother to email to tell you

Unfortunately, not all of us have perfect manners, and sometimes editors don't bother to respond if they're not planning on using an idea. I've even had an editor get quite shirty with me about this, claiming that I should know she wasn't interested in an idea by the fact that she hadn't got back to me. Just how I might be expected to judge the timescale of this rather unique rejection criteria without mind-reading skills I couldn't say. But sadly her magazine went out of business after a few months, and I'm sure it had nothing to do with being managed by an individual who didn't have the time management skills to deal in professional courtesy.

Generally, however, it's not so much that editors are rude, but that they don't like rejecting people. No one wants to tell someone else they can't use their work. So rather than send an email saying they don't want your ideas, they think it might be kinder simply not to respond. Although this comes from the nicest of motives, it goes without saying that's it's quite unhelpful to the professional freelancer. However, most editors don't mind a bit if you phone them up to clarify, and it's also a good chance to get an opening to send more ideas.

The importance of chase-ups

Once you start making regular chase-ups, you'll find they're not half as intimidating as you might have originally assumed. Not only are most editors nice, polite people, but you will find the incidence of your ideas having been genuinely considered for their potential very gratifying, and it should help you gain confidence. After you've made ten phone calls to editors you'd assumed had rejected you, and found that half have earmarked your ideas as potential winners, it should make you feel better about the whole process.

Chase-ups also lead to commissions. In my experience of perpetual pitching, I would say that less than half of editors respond within a month to the ideas I send them. This could be very discouraging if I was simply assuming the lack of response to be a rejection, and didn't bother to chase. But with regular chase-ups I've probably doubled the number of commissions I receive, simply because it's easy to underestimate how much editors need that nudge.

So rather than viewing chasing as the unpleasant task you'll do occasionally when there's nothing better on your agenda, give it the importance it deserves, and make it a proper part of your commitment to get into print.

How to chase

When you're in the position of a freelancer chasing an editor, it can be difficult to know the best approach. Chase aggressively and you'll annoy and dissuade editors from using you at all, but you don't want to appear under-confident in your ideas either. It's a tough balance.

The first thing to consider is getting the timing right when it comes to chase-ups. In my experience you want to be chasing an idea as regularly as you possibly can, without coming across as desperate or unprofessional. You don't want an editor to remember your name because you're always hounding them for a response to your pitches. But neither do you want them to forget you pitched them in the first place.

I would suggest that *two to three weeks after sending your ideas* is about right for a chase-up. The chances are that if you aim for two weeks you could get busy and it will stretch to three anyway, so use two as your ideal.

Not only is it important to get your pitching moving as fast as possible, but you also don't want to leave it too long to chase an idea. This greatly increases the chances of an editor having moved on, which of course undermines that valuable groundwork you put in introducing yourself and sending your ideas over in a timely manner. If you've pitched an idea to coincide with a season or issue, then you'll lose this advantage too.

REMEMBER: It's always better to pitch too late than too early.

Even though you don't want to leave pitching too long, for the most part it's always better to pitch – and chase – too late than too early. The latter could lose you a single potential slot if you're very unlucky, but the former will mark you out as over-enthusiastic for the foreseeable future. Few editors want to engage themselves with an overly pushy freelancer, so make it clear from the outset that you're not going to hound them.

Phone chase-ups work best

In the past, I used to send an email two weeks after pitching, politely explaining that I had sent some ideas and wanted to check if they had arrived with the necessary party. I think this is a nice way of saying you're not expecting a response immediately, but you're checking that your work has been received. This way you're also nipping problems like lost emails in the bud, so you don't risk missing out on placing a particularly timely piece due to a simple admin error.

Although I used to do this by email, I now make a phone call, and I do this for a number of reasons.

- If an editor has changed, or there is a general problem with an email address, then a chase-up email will go the same way as the original.

- Emailing gives an editor an excuse to put off responding, or to not respond at all. In contrast, making a phone call means that if you get through to the editor in question, they have to deal directly with you. Obviously they'd rather not be in the position of having to explain to someone on the phone that they've not got around to looking at some ideas (which is after all part of their job), so I find it tends to galvanise them into action much faster.

- You get more direct information. An editor will often fill you in on important facts, like when their next big supplement is out that you can pitch on, or when they will next be commissioning.

- They also might tell you less pleasing news too, like their budgets have just been cut, or their page count has been slashed. This isn't as bad as it sounds though, because at least you have the information to work with.

- The editor will know you're the kind of person who will call them directly if they don't get back to you, and this helps speed them up, too. I don't mean this in an aggressive or confrontational way, but most editors would rather avoid that phone call with a freelancer where they have to explain that they haven't looked at your ideas yet, or they don't like them.

So for all of these reasons I would suggest making a phone call rather than sending an email when you're chasing. Even if you don't get through to an editor, you can leave a voicemail and then send a follow-up email resending the ideas and mentioning your earlier call.

If it's a rejection following your chase, you've got it that bit faster, allowing you to send new ideas more quickly – thus speeding up the whole pitching process. The faster you get that pitching process turning over, the more chance you have of getting a commission, so it's a helpful thing to promote.

REMEMBER: **Professionals are generally very upbeat about being rejected.**

When you've been in the trade a while, rejection happens a lot, but more importantly it represents a new opening to send more ideas, which is a good thing. So take a tip from the pros and ensure that when you're talking to an editor who doesn't want to use your ideas, you make your voice sound like that's completely fine with you – even if you're not best pleased.

Won't editors resent me calling them in person?

In case you're unclear on this point, I will reiterate: editors may claim to be busy, they may claim to be on deadline, but they're not heart-surgeons or members of cabinet. No-one will die if their day's work doesn't get done, and editorial schedules are not as packed as they might have people assume. Most editors have plenty of time to go to a few lunches or make a few parties in a month, so they can fit in an extra phone call if they want to. An editor who is so busy that they can't spare five minutes to be courteous is either self-aggrandising or unable to manage their time effectively.

Reject those who continually reject you

You should also learn to be wary of expending too much energy on editors who keep ideas for months on end. The first time it happens I wouldn't let it bother you, as editors are often unsure about commissioning new freelancers, and will start getting back to you with gratifying speed once they've established you can produce work they want to publish. But if an editor routinely sits on your ideas for an aeon, you should start to consider if it is worth your while to keep pitching to them.

If you're looking to do this professionally, then you have to factor in a number of elements to what you're paid to write a piece. The time it's taken you to write the pitch in the first place naturally has to be added to the time you spend working on an article, and if you're routinely making ten or more phone calls just to get the piece commissioned, this is your paid-up time as well. In the long run it might not be worth the final pay to spend all that time chasing. Concentrate your efforts instead on regularly pitching editors who get back to you with reasonable speed – whether it's to reject you or otherwise. They're the ones who are offering you the steepest learning curve.

Of course there is also a point at which you should write off an editor who is rejecting all of your ideas – even if they're kind enough to do it in a timely fashion. Think about it as a score count which detracts from the money an editor is offering for the final piece.

REMEMBER: If a publication pays £300 for 1000 words that take you two days to write, but securing this commission has taken twelve pitches which took four days to write, the value of your final earnings dips considerably.

It's interesting to keep this dynamic in mind as you move into a more professional approach, as it can be surprising how often smaller trade titles can be a better use of your time in this respect. So whilst it's tempting to see the bigger pay cheque of the nationals and big consumer titles, don't forget the extra struggle to get onto their pages.

The lesson here is also one in patience. When you're starting out, you're naturally very eager to hear an editor's responses to your ideas and to get your work in print. After you've been sending ideas for a while you'll realise that many publications work to very slow timescales, and there can be an enormous gap between sending an idea and having it commissioned. This is why you'll be sending lots of different pitches to many different publications, so that you don't get too hung up on a certain batch of ideas. It's a funny thing with freelancing, but very often when you let go of an idea, mentally speaking, that's when a sudden slew of editors come back desperate for you to write it up for them.

Rejection – your golden opportunity to appear professional

Naturally, good chase-up practice is going to come with its fair share of rejections, especially when you first start out. This can be disheartening, but take note – rejection is yet another opportunity to impress an editor with your professionalism. React to rejection in the manner of a writer with plenty of experience and other opportunities at hand, and you'll up your chances of being commissioned next time around.

There are also some things you shouldn't do when an editor rejects your ideas. If you call an editor and they're not interested in your ideas, don't try to persuade them, argue with them, or in any way tell them they're wrong. Ultimately they know more than you do about what should and shouldn't go in their publication – and even if they didn't, it's entirely up to them what they decide to run.

Neither should you ask for some kind of feedback. This flies in the face of a lot of freelancing and career advice, which suggests that you should take the opportunity to learn from your mistakes, and an editor who has seen your ideas is ideally placed to help you in this fashion. But here's why it's a very bad idea in the feature-writing trade:

- It is a completely amateur thing to do and will mark you out as under-confident, and worse, unprofessional. A salesperson who hasn't sold a product to a customer doesn't return a few hours later asking for feedback on why the sale didn't work out. Neither do writers who have been in the trade for years phone up or email editors asking for advice on why such and such an idea wasn't right for a magazine. Asking for feedback will mark you out as a first-timer who is unsure of their abilities, and this impression will filter through to the editor, who is unlikely to want to commission someone with no experience.

- If you've done your research properly, your idea *should* be right for the publication, which means it will have been rejected due to one of several extenuating factors. This could be anything from they've run something similar recently to they suddenly ran out of space. Your job is to save an editor time, not put them in the position of being a teacher on your personal training course. They have enough to do.

- You may well get some kind of unsolicited feedback anyway if you're doing your chase-ups properly and contacting editors by phone. You'll be amazed, when you do this, just how often there is an impersonal reason why a particular set of ideas wasn't picked, and editors may also give you helpful advice unprompted. If they don't, thank them, and suggest you'll be sending some more ideas. Often their pleased response is good encouragement that your pitches were worth looking at.

- It often slows down or rules out the chances of editors getting back to you, and this is something you certainly want to avoid. I was talking with an editor I knew on a friendly basis, and she admitted that she rarely got back to writers who pitched her unsuccessfully because when she did so, they tended to ask for feedback, which she didn't have time to give.

There's no doubt that you will come up against a lot of rejection as a freelance writer, and for the most part you will also learn a lot from it. So try to see it as the excellent teaching experience which it is. It is crucial that you don't take it personally, either: as a seasoned professional with plenty of commissions I still get a reasonable number of ideas rejected. The number of commissions has gone up with my experience, but I still get more ideas rejected than I do taken up. The difference is that when you've been com-missioned a lot, you're not bothered if an idea's not right, because you know you're good at what you do.

REMEMBER: **Even professional freelancers get a large amount of rejection as part of getting published – they just don't see it as rejection anymore.**

Don't let the response of a particular editor get you down either. Some are more abrasive than others, and there are a few editors who think their subjective opinion serves as Gospel for everything in the print media world.

Learning the hard way: subjective rejection
I once sent out a batch of three ideas to three different editors on the same day, and rather unusually, within an hour one editor had come back commissioning one of the ideas, and two hours later a second asked for the same idea to be written up.

An hour later I received an email from the third editor telling me in no uncertain terms why the very idea which had just been commissioned twice that day (and, I might add, for considerably more prestigious publications than hers) would never work as a feature. Given that I'd secured two commissions on the back of that same idea, I was able to take her opinions very lightly indeed. But as I was starting out at the time, I wouldn't like to think how it might have affected my self-esteem if it hadn't been for those two other editors who liked the pitch.

It just goes to show that what works for one editor doesn't necessarily work for another, but that doesn't stop some individuals assuming their opinion to be the only one on the subject. I wouldn't go so far as to say ignore criticism – some can be valuable. But be very careful of mistaking the sniping of a stressed-out individual who's had a bad day for useful advice. Most editors, it should be added, will give you nothing but constructive feedback.

Meeting rejection with a happy voice and a pledge to send more ideas will go far in the eyes of most editors, and mark you out as someone with plenty of experience. So make the most of this great opportunity to paint yourself as a true freelancer.

A word from the editors

"Don't make a pest of yourself. Bombarding editors with messages every week is not the way to make friends. But most would be amenable to a quick hello every couple of months. You never know, you might catch them on a good day. You should never get disheartened if you suggest ideas to editors and they don't get taken up. They may simply not be in a position to commission you yet."

Andrew Williams, Deputy Editor, William Reed Business Publications

Keeping track of what you pitch

The pitching process is very much like a machine: you need to keep it ticking over with plenty of ideas and regular chase-ups, and once it's got going it has a bit of its own momentum. I mentioned earlier that it's in your interests to get this machinery working as fast as possible, but it's also important to keep careful track of the input and output.

Once you start pitching it will become obvious quite quickly that you need to keep track of who you're sending ideas to. If you've followed my advice earlier in the book and targeted a particular subject area, then the chances are you'll have a choice of a few different editors who can receive more or less the same ideas – rewritten carefully for their readership, of course. This being the case, if you don't keep track of who has received what, then you could risk putting yourself in the embarrassing circumstance of sending the same idea or ideas twice to an editor. Or missing out on pitching an editor with some great ideas because you're not sure if you've sent them already.

Knowing what you've pitched is also important for chase-ups. Editors will often ask you when you phone them to remind them of the ideas you sent through, so you'll want to have them readily to hand. With a good system for keeping track of who was sent what and when, you can also make the whole procedure more efficient, as well as build up valuable data on which editors get back to you quickly or commission frequently.

When you first start out it's easy to think you'll retain all this information in your head. After all, you're hardly going to forget an editor who has just given you a commission – right? You'd be surprised, however, when you start to get busy with writing, how you miss out on opportunities to keep very worthwhile editors in the loop if you don't have a system in place to highlight who's giving you good returns.

If this sounds complicated, it can be. Keeping track of who has received your ideas can be complicated when editors move and publications go in and out of business or shift publishing houses. Add to this the requirement to keep track of your invoices, and you're looking at a real need for efficient data storage. There are a number of ways to do this, and the solution you opt for will depend on your ongoing needs.

You may be thinking that all this admin sounds too involved (and boring) for your current requirements. But believe it or not, keeping track of your pitches with a degree of efficiency is what will lift your efforts above those of amateur would-be freelancers – and even a few seasoned professionals.

The written list

The simplest way to track pitches is to keep a written list of sorts. This is probably the most popular way in which freelancers keep track of the editors they're pitching, but it's by no means the best. It does have some obvious advantages, however. It's more or less immediate to set up and very easy to use. Most people use some kind of spreadsheet programme to keep their list on, which adds a bit of extra functionality when it comes to moving things around.

The thing to remember when using this type of data storage is that whilst it seems very immediate and usable, keeping it updated requires quite a lot of discipline and attention to detail. You need to be the kind of person who is very thorough in entering data, and is well able to put that next exciting pitch on hold to systematically log the details of what you've sent.

And it's quite a bit more work if you're aiming to go freelance long term, because you'll have to enter everything yourself by hand. Presumably you'll keep your pitches separately in Word documents using this system, so you'll have to open them up individually every time you want to send three ideas to a new editor, which involves a bit more time and effort as well. If you were to use a database, your pitches could be logged in text cells, making them easy to search for at a later date, as well as far simpler to collate three into one simple email.

If you're only really planning on getting one or two pieces in print for posterity, then this is probably the best method for you to use. Likewise if you're the kind of person who is good with methodical detail, but hates involved systems and computer programmes.

The basic database

You may choose to make use of an accessible database of the kind which often come free with software packages already on your computer system.

Aside from requiring no monetary outlay from you, these bring some of the functional elements into play to help maximise the efficiency of the data you store. It will take perhaps a day or two to get your head around one of these systems, but the benefits will be obvious immediately. Rather than house data on flat sheets, databases keep them in different tables which are interrelated. So you can have a table with the names of your pitches, a table with the names and contact details of editors, and one in the middle which combines the two and allows you to make meaningful links between the data.

As you can imagine, this makes it much simpler to identify which editors have received which pitches. There are also extra functions like automatic date entry, so you don't have to type in by hand the date when you sent an idea – the system will do it for you. If you're not so good at keeping efficient records, then this system will do some of the work for you and make it more likely that you house data effectively.

The advanced database

As the name suggests, this requires quite a bit more work and technical know-how. Don't be put off by this, though. Database systems can be self-taught fairly easily, or you can find out about taking a class in your local area.

You may think that this kind of system is only worth bothering with if you're planning on becoming a full-time professional freelancer, but in fact investing in a method for organising who gets sent what at this early stage can pay dividends.

As we covered earlier, chase-ups are the most oft-neglected and important part of the freelancer's job, and having the software to automate this process for you from the start can only bring you extra success.

With this in mind you might want to look out for more pro-fessional software packages to help you along the way. Think how much easier your motivation would be, for example, if a neat little program emailed you daily with a list of editors you were due to chase. Or was able to calculate the best response times and rates from editors and compile a list of 'first to pitch' leads. Not only would this make chase-ups simpler, it could also help you distance yourself from the emotional involvement of pitching certain titles, and logically assess which were delivering the best likelihood of publication.

The 'No Contacts' method has developed a database which can do all of these things. It is available to download as a resource from www.nocontactsnoproblem.com/database.html.

This database is unique in that it has been developed specifically to address the needs of fledgling freelancers. It keeps track of who you've pitched and when, draws up a list of who is due a chase-up, and even logs your articles and automatically sends out professional invoices once you've won your first commission.

It also has a system for calculating an editor's 'pitchability' rating based on how quickly and how often they respond to your pitches and chase-ups, and ranks them accordingly on a handy list of 'editors to pitch'. So if you're the kind of person who is good with creativity and not so hot on admin, this system could save you a lot of wasted pitches.

If I'm losing you with all the database talk, bear with me. I'm just trying to give you an idea that as a professional freelancer, chase-ups and keeping track of pitches effectively really is a key component of your success.

REMEMBER: Many, many people send ideas to editors. The ones who make it as professional writers are those who can follow up with a degree of professional efficiency.

> ### Web tip:
> If you're uncertain as to how to go about putting a database together, or why it can be of use, you can find out more at www.nocontactsnoproblem.com/database.html. There's also the facility here to download a ready-made database which has been custom-built for start-up freelancers.

Action plan

In these early days, when you're not busy writing com-missions, you have the perfect time to effect a proper system for keeping track of your work. Don't make the mistake of thinking you'll deal with this later. If you're using the 'No Contacts' method, it's vital you establish your effective chase-up practices now.

1. Choose a chase-up method which best suits the level of freelancing you intend to pursue.

2. Dedicate a full few hours to mapping out how your system is going to work for you, and what sort of functionality you need.

3. Buy the materials for whichever system you've chosen and build it to the best of your abilities.

4. Enter the details of the editors you've already pitched, and note if any need chasing.

8

Your first commission

By now the chances are you'll either have a commission in the bag or be very close to securing one. So it's only natural that you might be wondering how on earth you're going to land the thing when you've not the slightest idea how it all works. This chapter is designed to take you through the basic expectations of a commissioning editor, and to highlight any potentially scary questions which might come up in the process of being commissioned.

In this chapter, you'll:

- Find out how to maintain a professional front whilst accepting your first commission.
- Discover the vital questions you need to ask before you start writing – and know what not to ask.
- Cover basic issues of copyright and how to approach it.
- Understand how to deal with different types of brief.

Maintaining the professional front

If you've been following all the advice in this book, sending out dynamite pitches and chasing them up regularly, it's only a matter of time before you get your first commission. Feel free to jump around in excitement at this point.

A commission is great, but remember that your target is a printed article. If this sounds negative, it's not. Whilst a commission is a significant step towards getting into print, it's not a guarantee. By all means pat yourself on the back at this point and congratulate yourself on having come so far. But it's not time to celebrate just yet.

When you're starting out (and even when you've been freelance a while), there's still a small risk that an editor will change their mind, leave the publication, drop your piece in favour of a better advertising stream, or decide your final submission just isn't up to scratch.

You should also bear in mind after receiving a commission just how long it can take to get published. I would really advise against telling all and sundry that you're due to have a piece published in such and such national publication, because it may be a while before they get to see it. Save the celebrations for when you actually have your published article sitting on a newsstand.

Learning the hard way: an editor's word isn't always final
When I was starting out I sent several pitches to education pages on The Independent. *Only a few weeks later I picked up a message on my answer machine from the Education Editor, saying she was interested in commissioning a particular idea. Delighted, I returned the phone call which had been made only minutes before, but when connected with the editor found she had already changed her mind. The idea wasn't quite what she wanted after all. This has never happened since, and fickle behaviour of this kind is mercifully rare, but it just goes to show that you shouldn't necessarily consider a pledge for a commission as final.*

Phone or email?

So what forms can a commission take?

Your commission may well come as an email, in which case it's much easier to respond professionally. You'll want to demonstrate your enthusiasm by responding as soon as possible, of course, but you also have some time to properly draft your reply. My advice is to keep it very brief, as that's what most full-time writers would do. Agree to write it, say the deadline's fine, and generally communicate that you're pleased to be doing this for the publication.

But what happens if the phone rings, you pick up and a voice says: "Hello it's Mr Editor here from National Publication, I'd like to talk to you about these ideas you've sent me." What do you do?

Firstly, listen carefully and don't ask too many questions. My first phone call from a commissioning editor was from an employment editor at *The Guardian* who rang whilst I was writing up my university coursework in the public computer room. Suffice to say, I was somewhat overawed by the circumstances, but being in that room with all the other students probably worked in my favour and prevented me from saying too much and blowing the fact that I knew very little about freelance writing.

Learning the hard way: saying too much too soon

One of my favourite stories on this subject is about a small-time partnership of computer programmers who successfully bluffed their way into pitching for work with Apple Computers. It was an enormous project, and it was quite astonishing for them to have got onto this level, as they were up against mammoth companies who had been in the business for decades. Not only did their charisma carry them through to the final stages, the account manager all but told them they'd got the work at the closing minutes of their final presentation.

Seeking to seal the deal, one of the enthusiastic young entrepreneurs decided to speak up rather than keep quiet, and asked what would happen next, to which the account manager smiled and replied that this would be the writing of a purchase order – i.e. an invoice to accounts to pay for their services. At which point the young man asked, "What's a purchase order?"

Needless to say they didn't get the job, although the team in question went on to be a highly successful business, and now operate as business angels offering venture capital for other worthwhile start-ups.

If in doubt, keep quiet and make notes. You can always ask someone else what a particular term or phrase means later on. The other important aspect to remember is that as a freelancer you're here to save an editor time, not to add another trainee to their already busy workload. An editor uses freelancers to simply and painlessly delegate work outside their offices, so responding to a commission with a slew of time-consuming questions is going to eat into the efficiency of the process, not to mention probably causing the editor to doubt how competent you are to put the piece together.

If you really can't understand what an editor is talking about, ask (very politely) if they would mind sending you a brief by email.

Different types of brief

Editors vary enormously, and what constitutes a full brief for one publication won't for another.

- Some publications have a formula for sending out briefs, which editors adhere to when commissioning writers. This could have various sections like word count, pay rate, and other guidelines on how the publication usually operates. It might go so far as to detail a run-down of the typical reader, or cover a 'style sheet' which includes clarification on certain points of grammar or stylistic preferences for copy.

- Some editors will send you a list of questions which they'd like to see covered, and some (if you're lucky) will send you contacts they'd like to see used along with telephone numbers and emails. It goes without saying that if an editor goes to the trouble of sending you any such information, you should adhere to their notes as strictly as you possibly can.

- For the most part editors probably won't give you much of a brief. There's a kind of irony to this, as established writers normally find highly detailed briefs quite restrictive, and new-comers would prefer to have a lot of instructions written out. But often it seems that they come to you in reverse order, possibly because first-time writers are usually commissioned by busy editors who don't have time to thoroughly check credentials.

The moral of the story here is that an editor won't necessarily give you a full brief, and if they don't, it's perfectly normal. So you don't need to concern yourself with getting extra detail from them. Certainly when I started out I had very little in the way of instructions to write articles. So this means it's your job to properly research the slot you're writing for and confirm that your writing style adheres perfectly to the type of material they print.

If they do give you lots of instruction – use it! Sometimes you may not be able to use all the contacts on an editor's list because they have supplied you with far too many to feature, but for the most part, don't deviate from what they're asking. This may sound obvious, but when you've pitched with a certain angle in mind, and you're busy, it can be easy to follow your own trail through without consulting the editor's requests.

A word from the editors

"Submit your work in as complete a form as possible. That means everything spell-checked (manually, don't trust the computer), and fact-checked. We have sub-editors who will make sure nothing slips through the net, but as an editor, I always remember the writers who leave me and my team with the least work to do this end."

Victoria Ward, *Fortnum & Mason Magazine*

Asking the right questions

There are, however, some questions that are totally right to ask – indeed, you'd look rather unprofessional if you didn't ask them. Note, however, that even with very vital information about a brief it's not too strange to come back to an editor and explain that you forgot to ask for a particular detail. You're not really risking your professionalism by doing this. But you could be doing so by asking a silly question to which you should already know the answer – so take a double note. If in doubt, don't ask.

The following are questions you certainly should ask, if they're not automatically forthcoming.

Word count

That's it. Don't ask how many words should be spent on such and such a section – just ask for the number of words, plain and simple.

Very occasionally an editor will ask how long you think you can make your idea. If you're feeling confident, this situation offers you an opportunity to upsell. So an editor might ask, "How long do you think it could run to?", to which you reply that the topic could run to a considerable length, thus securing yourself the longest possible feature.

In terms of knowing the exact word counts of their paginations, however, you're not expected to carry this information in your head. An editor may sometimes forget this and ask you to write "two pages" or similar, but you still need to get a specific word number from them – that, or painstakingly count the length of a similar feature.

Pay rate

Always ask this before you start writing, as a professional writer would rarely start on a piece without establishing pay. There are some exceptions. If you're writing for a national newspaper, you can more or less assume that the pay will be to a set rate over which the editor has limited control (although they can often up it by a little). If the rate is below the expected minimums as set out by the National Union of Journalists, always point out this fact to the editor in question and ask for more. They may or may not be able to give you it, but it certainly won't damage your professionalism to be clear about expected rates of pay.

You may be thinking at this stage, "I'd write it for free, just to get in print." Remind yourself this is *not* a professional approach. Your time is money, and your writing a reflection of your valuable skill. Make sure you're seen in this category by the editor, and you'll maximise your chance of translating a commission into a printed article.

Remind yourself too of the value you placed on the last thing you were given for free. Are you as likely to use it as you would an item you'd lovingly chosen and paid for?

Deadline

Some editors will be a bit hazy about deadlines. I know some who say "in a few weeks"; what this usually means is that they prefer to be a bit ahead of themselves and have plenty of material ready to run. If they're not too bothered about you writing a piece to a particular deadline, it could be that they don't have a particular slot in mind, so time may run on a bit before you see your work in print. Far better is when an editor asks you to turn something around pretty quickly. This means they're quite desperate for a piece and your chances of getting it into print (fast) are much improved.

In the former situation, I would suggest you push a bit for a deadline and if it's not forthcoming, set your own and communicate it to the editor. It's for your own benefit to have a discrete timescale to work to, because otherwise it would be easy to let a piece drag on indefinitely as you strive to make it perfect. The other thing to remember is that an editor who doesn't give you a deadline may suddenly come back to you and ask if they can have a piece more quickly because a slot has come up for it, which is another reason to be as efficient as possible with your workload.

Whatever the editor suggests, agree to it immediately. It's your job as a freelancer to be 'can do'. This said, it's helpful to have an idea of what constitutes an average deadline, so you know whether your editor will be giving you some leeway or pushing you to rapid completion.

To a certain extent, of course, 'average' deadline length is entirely subjective. I have an editor who always commissions me to submit a piece in under a week – a pretty rapid turnaround by most standards. And I have other editors who check my availability and apologise for the tight deadline when they give me a month's notice. In my experience, the 'average' time is probably about three weeks. Magazines tend to give a month (although not always), and some may even give a month and a half or more.

In case you thought otherwise, feature writers practically never get deadlines of a few days or hours. This is more the kind of high-pressure circumstance of a reporter filing very short news items for a daily paper. So you don't need to worry about an editor coming back with an impossible target for a new writer.

When you're starting out, you won't know whether a deadline is a long amount of time or not, so it helps to be aware of the industry standards. If an editor gives you something to do in under a week, you should obviously do it to your best ability, but bear in mind that they have put you under the cosh in terms of timescale, so will probably be more forgiving of an error. More importantly, it usually means they have to get it in the publication fast, which is why when you're starting out, tight deadlines should be more appealing to you – they significantly increase your chances of getting into print.

Other issues

All editors and publications are different, and when you start out you won't have too much of an idea of what 'normal' behaviour is. But there are some circumstances in which when an editor commissions you, you may need to have some trickier conversations.

Box-outs

If the editor doesn't specify 'box-outs', and you notice that the section you're writing for always has boxed-out sections of text, you might ask if the word count includes this.

Quite often, editors don't state that they want smaller sections of text to break up the body as a whole, but when it comes to layout, designers need them – or the sub-editor is given the job of putting some in. So you can make their job easier by having them as part of the total word count. On a few occasions, an editor will come back to you after you've written a piece and ask for you to take some of it into box-outs. This can be rather annoying if they didn't state that they wanted them in the first place, so you may consider asking about box-outs before you start writing.

This is not a common circumstance, though. So if you're not sure if a section has box-outs – don't ask! You'll start the editor doubting whether you really know their section. Or make them think you want to be a bit too involved in the whole subbing process.

On-spec requests

Occasionally an editor might ask you to write 'on spec' if they identify you as a first-timer. This means that they see potential in you or your pitch, but they're not convinced that you personally can write it to a printable standard. Rather than risk putting their budget on the line, they'll ask you to gamble your fee for their approval and submit an article for free which they'll pay for if they like it. Magazines don't do this with professional writers, which in my opinion is a good reason to disguise as much as possible the extent to which you are new to the business.

If you find yourself in this position you may be tempted to submit an article for which you have not yet been guaranteed payment. There are two schools of thought on this:

- **It is a chance to prove yourself.** You might reasonably argue that an editor who has asked to see a piece 'on spec' has already expressed an interest in the idea, and is simply asking to see evidence that you can do it justice. As an excellent and motivated writer you should be more than well-placed to make a good job of it, so this would represent an opening for future assignments. For some writers, turning-out work 'on spec' has represented a valuable in-road to start selling their work to magazines.

- **It is a sign the editor doubts your ability.** The other view is that editors who are willing to put you to work for free are probably not too trusting of your ability to do the job in the first place. What's more, if they're not paying, they have far less incentive to print your work. An editor who has commissioned you (and hence promised you payment) is duty bound to pay you something – even if your work doesn't make print. That being the case they're far more likely to ask you to rewrite a piece which doesn't work for them, because otherwise they'll have to explain to their publisher why their commissioning judgement is poor enough to waste budget on an article which was never printed.

  In contrast, an editor who has got your work for free has no such obligation. In fact they can afford to look at it from quite the other way around. Not only will they be wondering whether to spend their budget on it, they'll probably have had doubts in the first place as to your ability (hence asking for it 'on spec') which tends to prejudice their reading of the finished piece. Think how differently you'd be likely to read an article which you believed to be written by a freelancer with twenty years' experience versus that of a writer whose work had never been in print.

Learning the hard way: 'on spec'

I personally find it very hard to put the same amount of dedication and professionalism into a piece which I have not been guaranteed payment for. It undervalues it in my eyes and tempts me to skimp on detail until the point at which I'm guaranteed payment. You might be more diligent than me, but I've always found money to be a strong motivator in writing top-quality work.

My best case in point is an incident with The Sunday Times Travel Magazine, whose editor asked for a piece 'on spec' which she subsequently deemed "nicely done, but a bit too food-focused for our pages".

Needless to say, had she been paying for the piece this would have been a case of a simple rewrite – a bit less on food, a bit more on the surrounding area. No problem at all for the average freelancer, who addresses this kind of simple matter regularly. In this instance, however, the editor had the option to reject the piece for the most cursory of reasons without putting her budgets at risk.

I went on to sell exactly the same piece to several other publications and counting (the article in question averages one sale a year).

I wouldn't want to rule out the on-spec route entirely for new writers. Just to point out that it is also possible to gain a proper commission for a fully paid piece without risking your time working unpaid.

Copyright

As a new writer, the idea of conversing with editors about issues of copyright may fill you with dread. It's not half as intimidating as it sounds, however, as most editors don't know too much about it themselves, tending to view whichever policy their publication runs with as the norm.

To give you a quick overview, as a freelancer, when you sell your work to a publication, *you automatically retain copyright*. This is how the situation should be, and it is vital to your success and income as a writer. What it means is that you have the right to sell or syndicate the same piece of writing to a different publication at a later date, thus greatly increasing the value of the work to you as the writer.

Standard rights procedures – First Serial Rights

For the most part, publications will have an agreement with writers that they get 'First Serial Rights'. This arrangement will often take the form of a written contract which is posted out to you, an email consent form which you agree to, or, very often, nothing at all, in which case your copyright is automatically assumed.

First Serial Rights means that a publication has the right to be the first to publish the work, and they often ask for syndication rights as well, in which circumstance they'll give you a cut if they sell the piece on. Some publications also ask that the piece is not published by someone else for a certain amount of time – usually three months.

At least fifty percent of the time (and more like ninety percent in my experience) a commissioning editor won't make any reference to copyright at all, in which case don't worry about it. The rights automatically pass to you, and no more needs to be said.

Some publications have a standard form which they'll wave at you, and for the most part this simply sets out fair practice on their part – although you should read it thoroughly to ensure that there are no back-door revocations of your rights.

Disreputable practices

Very occasionally publications operate rather disreputable techniques in order to deprive writers of their copyright, thus undermining their ability to make a professional living. The classic is to send you out a contract which looks like the usual writer's agreement, and is headed by the words 'you retain all rights', but on further reading reveals many other criteria which mean that technically, you don't.

Most notably, *The Times* tried to get away with this strategy in the late 1990s, until they were forced to back-track by continued protest by the National Union of Journalists. From a personal perspective, the only reason I can see why a publication would try to deprive a writer of their copyright is pure meanness. With the exception of a juicy news story, publications really don't benefit from being the sole publishers of a feature article – particularly since as it is reprinted, it is usually for a different readership.

What's more, the ability to reprint material can represent an important part of the freelance income, so to undermine this is to simply cripple the very professionals they're hoping to get the best out of. Very bad practice indeed.

In the instance of a publication which is set on you signing a particular form, be very wary. These are almost always the ones which demand you sign away total rights to publication. Ironically, in my experience these are also publications which don't tend to pay that well in the first place (and certainly not well enough to secure all rights to a feature), which rather confirms to me that it is an issue of penny-pinching.

Dealing with bad practice

So what do you do if you've received your first commission from a publication which suddenly demands all rights? Obviously, in this delicate circumstance I wouldn't advise refusing to write the piece, or even making much of a fuss. Instead I would suggest that you *simply ignore the form.*

I've done this on many occasions, and have even had one publication go so far as to chase me up and say they couldn't pay me without the signed form. But I ignored this too, and they did pay me, and then conveniently forgot about the form.

It seems to me that publications may try it on in this respect, but they won't necessarily carry any threats through to fruition, because they know that actually, what they're asking is unreasonable. In addition, editors are usually on the side of the writers in this circumstance, as it will commonly be the publisher's decision to try and intimidate writers out of their syndication rights. Such behaviour will probably already have led to protest by writers. So they may well silently disregard your flouting of the rules.

Pictures

Some publications will try and secure a few pictures along with an article, and will ask you to source them when they're commissioning. This is a bit of a vexed issue amongst journalists, because in theory publications shouldn't really ask. After all, your freelance fee covers the writing of the piece, not the duties of a picture editor or photographer. But in practice it's often easier for you as the writer to source a few pictures whilst you're in direct contact with your experts.

Again, it's usually magazines with smaller budgets who request images. Newspapers like *The Times* have generous photography budgets, and probably picture editors too, who would in no way want their creativity hindered by second-rate press shots supplied by a writer. But magazines where an editor is acting as a picture editor as well may try and take some of the strain off by delegating to a freelancer.

There's something of a balance to be struck here in how you handle the request. If an editor is asking you to simply scout around for a few publicity shots whilst you're writing the article, I personally think there's no harm at all in obliging. In fact I'm willing to bet money that in this circumstance, the freelancer who comes through regularly with good images rapidly becomes a favourite of an overworked editor.

Your ethics vs the publisher's

But here's the rub. There is a code of ethics which states that writers shouldn't supply pictures and photographers shouldn't supply copy. There are exceptions to this rule – travel journalism, for example – but for the most part writers and photographers are supposed to respect one another's patch and leave the experts to do it properly. This is probably more important than ever now that anyone can take a half-decent shot with a digital camera, and publications can squeeze photographers' incomes by having writers supply passably printable pictures.

You may have your own feelings on this, but personally, wherever possible, I'd prefer someone who has dedicated their career to training in photography and is passionate about getting a great shot to do their work. Particularly when the alternative is me snapping away without a clue what I'm doing, purely in order to put more money into a publisher's pocket.

Striking a balance

As you might already have discerned, however, there is clearly a balance to be struck, and for the most part that balance is all about good communication. There's a big difference between agreeing to help an editor out by sourcing a few pictures where possible, and supplying a full complement of professional pictures free of charge. Pictures are a real pain to work with, as they take time to source, upload and download, and photographers have all manner of special arrangements to do this at high speed. So if you agree to send twenty pictures, you're adding on a few extra hours of work for no extra pay – hardly the behaviour of a seasoned professional.

If an editor is asking you to supply lots of pictures, or acting as if pictures are a reasonable part of your fee, then there's nothing wrong in gently reminding them that according to the National Union of Journalists' code of practice you shouldn't be supplying pictures at all.

There are one or two low-budget magazines which rely heavily on pictures, and actually set out in the brief that the writer supplies 'x' amount of pictures. Unfortunately there's not much you can do about this; if you take the brief on, you have also agreed to the pictures. But for the most part, you should only agree to source a few pictures dependent on whether your contacts can easily supply them.

Expenses

Unless your piece involves some necessary train or car travel somewhere in the UK, it's unlikely that you'll need to know about expenses. You may see them mentioned on a commission, but they usually relate to a story whereby some sort of travel was an unavoidable part of the piece. An example might be that you had to go up in person to see the workings of a particular piece of equipment, or experience something first-hand for a story.

For feature writers, however, this is quite rare. Most interviews can be done over the phone or by email, and anyway, you'll want to avoid claiming for expenses wherever possible. Editors have limited budgets which run out each month, and they're probably not going to keep commissioning a writer who eats up a portion of that money with expense claims.

Ironically, for travel features you can't claim for flights or travel at all – even though you may be covering distances which involve expensive modes of transport. But generally there will be other ways to cover this cost, which we'll come to in Chapter 11.

The 'can do' attitude – yes to everything

When you're in the process of being commissioned, you really do want to make yourself as agreeable as possible. With the exception of the unusual circumstances outlined above, agreeing first and working out what you're going to do second is not a bad way to operate. Inevitably, the pressure and excitement of confirming that commission will see you move mountains to deliver the piece on time.

Learning the hard way: nothing's impossible

When I was starting out I routinely got hold of contacts or facts which I thought were literally impossible to track down – based, I think, on sheer determination to get into print. After all, getting the story together is the easy part – it's getting the commission which is tough.

I've interviewed people from pay-phones in foreign countries at 2am, and set my alarm for 4am in order to file copy on time. But compared to chasing and pitching editors, a bit of extra effort to deliver the goods is no big thing.

Web tip:
If you've been commissioned and are looking for some extra advice, try the online forum at www.nocontactsnoproblem.com/forum.html. You can get advice here on tricky issues, and anonymously post questions you'd rather not ask your editor.

Action plan

After you've read this chapter through, have a quick recap of the major topics which you might come up against. Try to commit them to memory as far as you are able. Then, ensure that you put them into practice when that vital commissioning phone call or email comes your way.

9

Writing the thing

You're approaching the final hurdle, which is simply to ensure that your submission is of a high enough quality to make it past the eagle-eye of the editor and end up being allocated a slot in a publication. With all the work you've done so far it's still possible to make a mistake or two here, so stay focused on the quality of your work.

In this chapter, you'll:

- Understand the basic expectations for freelance feature content.
- Find out how to track down sources and integrate their comments into your feature.
- Know how long you should spend writing your feature.
- Discover how to supply print-quality pictures in the right format.

Don't worry – this isn't one of those chapters full of common-sense opinion on how to write good features. Here we cover the bare bones of what an editor will expect to see in a feature, and how to supply that content with minimal effort and maximum efficiency. We'll also look at how long you should be spending on a certain word count based on how much you're being paid.

Don't panic – it's not too difficult to write articles

Once you've got your commission in the bag, and you're ready to write the piece, you may well be feeling a combination of elation and blind panic. On the one hand it's extremely exciting to have won your first commission, but on the other, the pressure of writing an article to the standard of a national publication is quite daunting.

To reassure you on this point – it's not too difficult to write articles. In fact you will have probably already covered the requirements of supplying press-quality articles if you've done some or all of the following:

- Produced presentations or speeches for work purposes.
- Written marketing material, brochures, website copy or other written copy in the course of your job.
- Been to university or are currently on a university course.

Plus, if you've picked up this book and have read to this stage, I'm assuming that you have confidence in the standard of your writing, and this usually presents itself in whatever position you happen to find yourself.

Looking for more compelling evidence that you have the ability to produce material to this standard? If you've won a commission, you've already done it. When you submit a well-written pitch which an editor wants to commission, you've proved your writing to be of publishable merit.

REMEMBER: **Once more with feeling. If you've submitted a winning pitch, you've already proved you can write to the standard of the publication that is commissioning you.**

Don't get hung up on issues of literary genius, either. Most newspaper and magazine articles are sold on a compelling topic rather than beautiful prose. The average person doesn't pick up a newspaper to immerse themselves in good writing; they do it because they want to read good stories, or find out about topical issues. So your main goal as a writer is to communicate your great idea with lots of interesting facts and quotes to back it up. In fact a sizeable portion of the text you submit will be other people's words – carefully selected and edited, of course, to make a nice, smooth-flowing piece.

How long should I take?

This is often the first issue to trouble new writers – even before they've started worrying about what the content of their article should be. It's an important issue, because in my opinion you can actually sabotage the content of your piece if you spend either too little or too much time on it.

Not enough time speaks for itself, and I would never assume that you would make this mistake on a first commission. But too much is much easier to do, especially when you're being paid a freelance fee which can seem quite high. If you put too much time into a freelance article it's not the end of the world, but you'll almost inevitably end up with far too much content, which you'll then be desperate to cram in to demonstrate all the fascinating detail you've found out.

When you do this, it's easy to enter into that 'wood for the trees' type of writing, where you inadvertently obscure the main points your article is making, simply because it's tackling far too many angles. I've certainly done this before, where I've got so carried away with detailing hard-hitting facts to support the article that I haven't properly explained the tenets of the topic in the first place, and an editor has asked me to go back and clarify points which should have been very obvious at the start of the piece.

On the up-side, you do tend to get better material this way, and if you're a very ruthless editor of your own work, you may end up with dynamite pieces. But you will also be doing extra work unnecessarily, which is not a great model for going on to a proper professional role. So rather than getting into the habit of under-paying yourself for your time, it's better to aim for efficiency where possible.

When you first start writing I guarantee that you will do too much work – it's unavoidable because you'll be so enthusiastic to do a good job. The question is what you should be aiming to achieve in the first place. So here's a straightforward breakdown.

- For an average article of 1000 words in length, a magazine or newspaper would envisage you spending around two days writing it up. *But –*

- A new writer who has never tackled this kind of market before should probably be aiming to spend around four days on a 1000-word piece.

To an extent you can scale this up or down, but you have to allow slightly more time proportionally for shorter pieces, and a little less for longer ones.

Considering that an article of this length would be paid (according to NUJ averages) £230, this may seem like quite a short amount of time to be earning that much money (unless you've come from the corporate world, where it will probably seem an abysmal daily rate). It should be added that once you've been freelancing for a while, you'll probably be able to produce a 1000-word article in less than two days. Certain pieces you can even knock out in only a few hours if you've researched them already, or they don't require quotes, like travel pieces.

In the case of your first piece, however, you'll want to spend more than two days, and I would suggest spending a working week – spread out over three weeks if possible. Think of it as a training exercise which you're lucky enough to get paid for. Many people spend thousands going to journalism school to learn these skills, and you now have the opportunity to practise them in a professional context for a slightly lower rate.

In my experience when it comes to writing, people's core ability doesn't improve much with practice, but their speed and proficiency does. So if you know you can write, spending a long time researching, writing, and going over your text several times will ensure that you're presenting your abilities in the best possible way. Ultimately, you'll know when you've finished a piece which is good enough to go into print, and the more you practise, the faster you'll get.

Establishing the tone of your feature

Now that you've worked out how long you should spend on a piece, your next issue will probably be what kind of style to write it in. As I mentioned earlier, to an extent you've already mastered this in your winning pitch, but it's also important to make sure the right tone flows through your entire feature.

I've found that the simplest way to do this is to identify the section you're writing for, and read it through twice before you start writing to cement the 'tone' in your head. Some voices will come easier to you than others, and will usually depend on which media you read most commonly.

Learning the hard way: tabloidese
Personally I find broadsheet writing comes quite naturally, but I sometimes have to rethink my style for consumer magazines. Tabloids are also a bit harder for me – I usually write out the piece as best I can and then go over it in my head in a local accent to pick up any bits which would sound strange in dialect. If this sounds like an unusual way of tackling tabloidese, try reading a sentence or two from a broadsheet, and then do it in a strong regional accent. It has the effect of drawing attention to awkwardly highbrow words and phrases, and a more natural 'dialect' tends to present itself.

You may find that a particular style of writing comes very easily to you, and I would suggest that this style should be the publication genre to which you send the majority of your pitches. You'll probably know innately what this should be anyway.

What should go into it?

This is probably one of the trickier questions confronting first-time writers. If you've won a commission based on your pitch, then you'll already have a vague structure mapped out. But that doesn't mean you have the slightest clue about who you should be speaking to, or what your content should focus on.

Incidentally, if your pitch has relied on rather more creative thinking than factual, you don't need to worry too much. I'll reiterate here that most editors don't mind if you don't stick rigidly to the bullet points you outlined in your pitch, and quite often you'll find your piece naturally takes a particular direction in the course of your research. That's what a pitch is, after all – a commitment to research an interesting topic. It would be rather unfair of an editor to expect you to have put all the work of researching a piece in before you've even written it.

So what kind of content should you be supplying for an article? Publications vary, but in terms of what a standard feature covers, here's a simple breakdown of typical content.

Newspaper, factual article, 1000 words

One piece of factual research or finding
Preferably from a university or other recognised research body, but statistics from a company are also OK. You can also add a quote from whoever carried out the research to add an extra insight into the findings.

One quote from a 'case study' person supporting the research
This is different from the person who carried out the research, or someone who simply lends their voice to supporting it. It should be someone who evidences the findings by their behaviour or circumstances. So in the case of research which shows that people are working longer hours, it should be a person who can explain how the last few years have seen them spend longer at the office. Generally, this person should be your 'Average Joe' – a member of the public with whom most people can identify, to form your primary case study.

One quote from a professional person
By professional, I mean in some kind of reasonably important capacity. It could be an employer, a doctor, a lawyer, or someone from a professional body like a university. Again, they should not be involved in the original research, but should be clearly able, by their role, to offer a worthwhile opinion on the subject. In the case of changes to the law, for example, someone from the legal profession would be ideal, whilst a medical topic would naturally call for a doctor or similar (medical doctors are hard to get hold of).

One quote from a professional person from a different viewpoint
In the course of interviewing a few people and professionals, you'll almost certainly find that the 'different viewpoint' naturally occurs. People are very interesting, and even if someone is more or

less parroting what another professional has said, they inevitably add a different angle which you hadn't considered. This can be a useful way to round-up your piece too, by suggesting a different stance or view which hadn't previously been thought of.

This is a very formulaic approach, and I would encourage you to develop your own style if it suits you better. If you're really anxious about what to include, however, this format will give you the bare bones of a well-researched piece – all you need to do now is string it together convincingly.

You should also bear in mind that this is the format of a *factual* newspaper or magazine article – the kind of thing which addresses a topic like education or employment, or similar. At the risk of insulting your intelligence, this wouldn't work for a consumer title, where articles are generally heavier on case studies and lighter on quotes.

REMEMBER: **For a consumer article, you usually need to halve the quotes, or dispense with them altogether.**

If we're talking about, say, a health article to go in a women's magazine, you would probably want one case study to talk at length about their experiences, and a doctor or similar to do likewise. For a first-person travel article you may not need any quotes at all, because you are the case study quoting for the entire piece. But use your common sense and see what the articles have done before.

It may help you out a lot at this stage to have a formula for the content and composition of an article. In general, the logical way to approach writing an article goes something like this:

- Consider what you want your article to cover, and draw up a list of the people and experts you need to source in order to do justice to your topic.
- Identify those experts and get in touch with them, explaining your topic and asking to establish a time to interview them.
- Interview them.

- Consider how the material you've gathered will flow smoothly into an interesting piece, and if necessary draw up a short plan.
- Write your article.

The key is first to establish your expert 'slots', and to fill them. You may not get hold of every expert you had in mind first time around – people go on holiday or are otherwise unavailable for all kinds of reasons – so replace them where necessary with similar experts or case studies.

A factual newspaper or magazine article hangs on the quality of its quotes, so make sure you have a comprehensive number without having to curtail your people's genius comment due to overcrowding.

To give you an idea of how many quotes you'll need in numbers:

- A 500-word factual piece would need around two: quotes, statistical data, case studies, or expert opinion.
- An 800-word piece should have around three.
- 1000 words needs about four.
- 1500 should have about six.

You can get away with less than this, and I've seen 1000-word articles with just one or two people to quote. In general, though, it would rather undermine the non-partisan nature of your article to have so few. A well-rounded piece needs contrasting viewpoints.

How long is a piece of string?

Obviously, when an editor gives you a word count you should stick to it – and if they don't give you one, ask. Magazines and newspapers have very specific slots for articles, and they require certain word counts which are rarely altered. Which is yet another good reason why you should never just send in a finished article as your pitch.

You do have a little bit of leeway in terms of length, but only a little. If you've been to university or college you may remember that assessed work can be 10% either over or under the maximum, and the same applies to print media. It goes without saying that you shouldn't really be under, though – the editor should feel they're getting their money's worth. Don't go over the 10% either. Publications really can't adjust their page count to factor in your literary stylings, so don't annoy the staff by making them edit huge sections of your work. Submitting to the right length is your job.

If you're *really* desperate to include something which takes you more than 10% over, I would suggest that you highlight a section which can easily be cut, and explain this to the editor when you send the work over. That way if they have the space for the extra text they can include it, but if they (most likely) don't, it will be no problem to cut the chunk you've highlighted.

Generally though, stick to the word count. I've spoken to editors whose main bugbear is writers who continually submit work which is much too long.

Interviewing

This is really just another word for 'having a conversation with someone whilst paying careful attention to what they're saying'. And as you probably do this every day, you don't really need many hints on how to conduct a good interview. What I will say, however, is when starting out, writers normally overestimate the time they need to spend interviewing. For the purposes of providing some comment for an article, a ten-minute interview is fine. It's only if you're writing out a case study which consists of comment alone that you'll need longer. It also depends on how verbose your subject is, of course: some people reel off superb sound-bites from the minute you pick up the phone, whilst others would rather not be saying anything at all.

For your first pieces you may feel more secure recording interviews, playing them back, writing them out in full, and then picking out comment that is relevant to your piece. As you become more confident you may well find that taking notes whilst the person is talking is quite adequate to allow you to extract the most compelling quotes and save yourself all that transcribing and editing.

A word from the editors

"Don't just rely on the usual tried-and-tested contacts. Use your own sources, and dig out some really interesting comment. I'd also encourage people to wear out some shoe leather if possible, and meet contacts face to face. It makes for much better interviews."

Jan Goodey, Journalist and Journalism Course Leader,
Brighton & Hove City College

Getting good pictures

If you've been asked to supply pictures and you're not *au fait* with this area of print journalism, there are a few things you should know.

Firstly, there are a large number of organisations which are not only happy to supply you with good-quality pictures for free, but are in fact very eager to get their pictures published. These are companies who have some kind of picture resource as part of what they regularly supply to the press.

Examples of this might include:

- A hotel that has taken publicity shots of its lovely bedrooms.
- Bars that take pictures of their beautifully presented drinks.
- Retailers who have product shots of what they're selling.

If you're after any of these sorts of pictures, it should be plain sailing – although I would still advise you to ensure that you're not being exploited financially in the supply of images, or inadvertently cheating a photographer out of his or her hard-earned trade. Then contact the press department of the relevant organisation – or even better, their PRs (a resource we come to in the next chapter). They will send you over pictures which have already been approved for print quality.

Case-study pictures

It can be slightly more awkward when an editor asks you to supply pictures of case studies. I hate it when they do this, because I always feel bad that some nice person has given up their time to talk to me for free, and I repay them by asking for another favour. Surprisingly, though, case studies tend to be extremely accommodating about this, and I have never had a problem getting hold of pictures. I suppose the one advantage for your interviewee is that they get to police the image which goes out, rather than having a photographer show up and snap their worst angle.

Size matters

The problem that sometimes crops up in this instance is that the picture is too small or of too poor a quality to go in a magazine. Most editors will ask for 'high res' pictures, which is another word for 'big'. Pictures need to be a certain size to go into print, otherwise stretching them to the relatively big page spaces makes them look blurry and dreadful. The 'resolution' basically refers to the amount of digital information held per square inch of the picture.

REMEMBER: **For print, the minimum DPI, or 'dots per inch', resolution must be 200.**

There's no way around this. You can make a picture larger in dimension using imaging software, but you can't add information which isn't there, and if the DPI is too small, scaling up will downgrade the quality and your picture won't be printable. Unfortunately, if a case study or someone else supplies you with a little picture like this, the only thing you can do is ask them if they have one at a higher res. The only exception is if the picture is medium resolution, but enormous in dimension, in which case it can be scaled down to a higher spec. If pictures aren't your thing and this sounds confusing, look for the size of the file: if it's pretty big – 500MB or more – you'll usually be OK.

If you've not really used imaging programs, you may be wondering how on earth you'll know if an image is of the required resolution. You can check the size of an image by right-clicking on the icon and looking at its properties. Unfortunately, though, in order to check the DPI in the case of pictures you're uncertain of, you really do need a professional-quality imaging program like Photoshop (the industry standard in print media) or Jasc Paint. If you have this program you just open up the file and look up the image properties on the tool bar; it will give you a run-down of the resolution and other related data. Sometimes you can also right-click on the icon of an image, and it will bring up a menu which includes size information if your computer has other software which allows you to read it.

Far less of an issue, but also relevant, is the format in which the image comes.

REMEMBER: Print images must be supplied as a Jpeg, a Tiff or a Giff.

This means they have been compacted to a high quality for easy moving about, in a standard format readily understood by all imaging programs. You'll know if an image has been saved in this way, because it will show up as the file extension – image.jpg, for example.

Most people nowadays will supply images in this format; in fact, the way in which digital cameras are set up makes it quite hard not to. But occasionally an image will come across as something different like a Bitmap, in which case you'll have to ask for the Jpeg, Tiff or Giff format.

You may know most of this already, but it's very important you understand that terms like DPI are standard across print media. Under no circumstances should you be extra helpful by asking an editor what size and format they want an image – you should know already because it's common knowledge in the sector.

Web tip:
Writing takes practice, but half the battle for freelancers is reading what it is the editor wants to arrive on their desk.
For editors' tips on great articles, logon to
www.nocontactsnoproblem.com/editorstips.html

Action plan

By now you should have sent a few of your carefully crafted pitches out to well-chosen editors, and either be well on your way to receiving a commission, or have received one already. Keep the vital tenets of putting features together in mind when you write your pitches, and have them to refer to when it comes to writing up your first commission.

10

Keeping 'em coming

Got the first commission in the bag and looking to capitalise on it for regular work in the future? This chapter covers the next steps in freelancing – going from one or two articles in print to making publication a viable source of income. More importantly, we also look at what happens after your article has been submitted, as the long slog is not quite yet over.

In this chapter, you'll:

- Understand how to begin moving from occasional commission to regular work.
- Find out about rates for the job, pay issues and how to negotiate like a pro.
- Discover what happens after your work has been accepted.
- Learn how to deal with requests for rewrites.

Don't give up your day job ...

If you've got this far and followed the steps in this book, then it's time to give yourself a pat on the back, because you're well on your way to seeing yourself in print – or perhaps you have already been published.

You've now learnt how to properly scope the market, put together dynamite pitches, send them off, and chase them up like a true professional. And provided you keep the cogs turning and the ideas churning out, then your name in print is a foregone conclusion.

At this stage you should remind yourself of why you're putting in all this work, and reassure yourself as to what's been achieved so far. Think how much more you know about the print process now, and mentally recall some of your best ideas – you're still learning, but you've come a long way.

You may have also encountered some rejection or feelings of self-doubt when sending out your ideas to editors. This is perfectly normal, and is just part of the process of getting into print. But if you've managed to stave off any such negative feelings, then that's great.

Whilst the beginning part of assessing your goals and brain-storming ideas is exciting, you're now entering the part of the process which feels more like a long slog, because you're in the phase of continually sending ideas, chasing editors, and coming up with new pitches to send out. Don't give up! This stage is one of the hardest, but if you're determined to get into print then it sorts the dedicated professional from the talented hobby-writer.

If you're aiming to become a full-time freelancer, this isn't the time to stop your day job. Many people leave their full-time job to go freelance, hoping it will give them the impetus to succeed. In theory, at least, there's no motivator for getting into print like needing to pay your rent on time. I'm not saying that this strategy won't work, but there is a far less stressful way of becoming a full-time freelancer.

The downside is, like most good things in life, the process takes a bit of patience. So whilst you may be gearing up to become a full-time writer, you should understand that it takes time – particularly if you're coming at it with no contacts. Every editor you approach will essentially be a cold call, and you'll have no established relationships with staff who can easily say, "Oh yes – I know him or her, they've worked in a professional publishing capacity."

This isn't necessarily a disadvantage. Remember that most free-lance journalists have spent years establishing themselves in lowly staff jobs first before even getting a position where they can write. So if you're coming to the process cold, you're saving yourself at least five years of nine-to-five grind. This being the case it may naturally take a little longer to establish yourself as a professional name, but I guarantee you it will be much quicker than the traditional route.

Think of it as a training period which comes with the added advantage of paying some money whilst you're moving towards a full salary.

How long does it take to go pro?

What everybody wants to know when they start is – how long? How long until I'm earning a decent wage? How long before these ups and downs of income even out? How long before I know for sure I can make enough money doing this?

These are hard questions to answer, as much depends on the amount of work you put into the process. I'm afraid the answer is usually double the time you think it should take, and a little bit more besides. This is particularly true in the case of knowing for sure that you can make a good living. You probably want more clarity than that, so I would say perhaps a year to get yourself to a situation where you are on a tolerable but low wage. And another few years to get your income up to a level appropriate for a skilled professional.

The good news is that when you're not earning a full-time wage, journalism isn't a full-time job, which leaves you free to supplement your income in other ways. What's more, it's a very flexible and easy job to integrate into your life. Even if you're working full-time in another position, you can scope out a few editors on your lunch break, brainstorm ideas on your way home, and write up your pitches in the evening. When your first commission comes through I guarantee that you will make the time to write up a really good piece.

Learning the hard way: from student to freelance writer
I started pitching freelance ideas when I was a student, which obviously gave me more flexibility to manage my time – especially as I was studying an arts subject. But I have also worked full-time jobs whilst freelancing, and managed to keep on top of pitching and writing whilst doing the odd stint on a magazine quite far into my career. It can be done. And once you've got the mechanism working smoothly, and learned a few things about what kind of ideas editors go for, you'll be in a position to scale down your other income source and eventually dispense with it altogether.

The sordid topic of coin – how much should I be paid?

If you're thinking about making a full-time living as a freelancer, then obviously issues of pay will concern you greatly. Luckily, whilst many issues to do with professional writing tend to be rather subjective, pay has been neatly tackled by the National Union of Journalists.

The NUJ has thoughtfully drawn up a list of expected minimum pay for freelance work, which is available for anyone to view on their website, and generally recognised as standard throughout the industry. It breaks publications down into type according to what kind of advertising revenue they might attract:

- A big consumer title like *Vogue* would be right at the top for the enormous income they make from all that designer advertising.

- A small trade publication like *British Baker Magazine* would be limited to the inexpensive advertising sought by very niche producers of food manufacturing equipment or similar.

On this basis, the NUJ expects publications to pay in proportion to their own income, so the suggested minimum rate for a publication like *Vogue* might be double that of *British Baker*. The lowest acceptable figure for any publication is around £230 per 1000 words, which is a very reasonable sum for the labour involved.

Unfortunately, whilst the NUJ decides and publishes these figures, publications are in no way bound to them – and some pay significantly under what should be reasonably expected of them. On average, however, most will pay roughly within the minimum rates, allowing you to make a decent living.

Negotiating your fee

The other good thing about the published rates is that they provide an industry standard which you can refer editors to when negotiating a fee. Always ask what the fee will be upfront, and if it's below the expected minimum *always, always point it out and ask for more money*. You will be doing a disservice to your own professionalism, not to mention other freelancers, if you don't.

If an editor won't budge and the fee is not too far short of the minimum, then I think it's OK to accept – but you might want to temper your acceptance with some kind of proviso such as: "I'm happy to do this piece for that amount, but perhaps we can talk about increasing the sum for other work I do for you once you've seen the quality of my writing." Most editors will agree to this, and you're in a stronger position to ask for extra money once you've got a track record as a good writer.

Don't make the mistake of thinking you'll make yourself more attractive to editors by agreeing to be underpaid. For the most part the priority of the commissioning party is to delegate work to a strong writer who will add a great story to their publication. Saving money comes a poor second to that, and is mostly influenced by the publisher, who sets the budgets.

A habit of less experienced editors is to ask you how much you charge. This is a silly question, as clearly you will be charging different rates depending on who you're writing for, and every editor should know that. It's also rather an unfair tactic to try and get you to state your price first, placing you at a disadvantage in the negotiating procedure.

In case you weren't aware, when you're discussing payment in any business setting, *the person who names the price first is always at a disadvantage.* Wherever possible you should avoid placing yourself in this position. When an editor asks you what you charge, the temptation is to name your minimum rates so as to avoid pricing yourself out of the market. However, you may find they're willing to pay more than you expected. In this circumstance I usually reply by explaining that I charge different amounts depending on the budget of who I write for. I then add that whilst my fees vary, I'm sure their budget is set, and furthermore, they'll have an idea already of what they pay their writers. So could they please let me know the average they pay for the word count they've suggested?

Most of the time an editor will come back with a figure in this instance, leaving you free to accept it if it's OK, or to ask for a little more if it's below NUJ rates. Ironically, I've found that the publications which ask you to state your fees usually pay a little bit over the minimums. The ones which pay substantially less often admit their substandard fees outright, to save the embarrassment of you accepting the commission and then refusing it once you see the fees.

Tougher editors

Sometimes editors will refuse to give you a figure, and this is often when they're commissioning for the first time themselves and have no precedent on which to base fees. They should still have a budget, though, so you can (gently) push them to reveal how much they have to spend and how many articles they should be able to get out of it. This is not ideal, as it's a little intrusive. But it's also your livelihood we're talking about, and an editor who isn't professional enough to have set rates for their writers simply isn't playing fair.

Remember too that whilst £10 or £20 extra for an article might not seem like a large amount of money, it soon adds up if you go on to write a lot of articles for a particular publication. I write about two articles a month for a publication from which I negotiated an extra £20 per 1000 words. This earns me an extra £700 or so a year – not a vast sum, but not bad for a few minutes' work. In fact, negotiating more money per word count is absolutely the fastest way you can make money as a freelancer.

Rewrites

After you've submitted a piece, your job isn't quite over. For the next few weeks you need to be available by phone or email in case an editor has any questions. Incidentally, more than one editor I've spoken to actually rates writers on how readily they're available *after* they've submitted a piece. Editors may need to check facts, contact a case study for a photo, or simply quickly query the way in which you've worded something.

REMEMBER: **Making yourself available during this time will cement yourself as a professional in the eyes of an editor.**

You can imagine how frustrating it must be to have a deadline looming, and the only person who can answer a particular query is uncontactable.

Unless you are gifted with a rare combination of writing ability and ESP, you may well be called upon to make a change or to rewrite a piece at some point. At the risk of stating the obvious, this just means that your first attempt at the article wasn't quite right, and you need to change the content a little (or a lot). Requests for rewrites are reasonably rare – particularly if you're writing for an editor who lives on tight deadlines.

When you start out, however, an editor may want to play it safe and not allocate a slot for your work before they've had the chance to see what kind of material you'll submit. Unfortunately, this makes it more likely that an editor will ask for something to be changed, because they've already allowed for this possibility. In addition, as a first-time writer your enormous drive to submit excellent work can make you misjudge things in terms of content and relevance.

The key with rewrites is *not to take it personally*. The natural response when you're starting out is to assume that a rewrite request is a direct criticism of your personal writing abilities. Whilst it does obviously mean that you haven't submitted quite what a particular editor is looking for, you shouldn't underestimate how much this happens, even with their seasoned freelancers who have been writing for them for years.

Certain editors see the commissioning process as more fluid than others, and whilst you'll have plenty who take your work without questioning it, some almost seem to look upon your submission as a first draft in a collaborative process in which they hammer out what they really want. It's not personal, and in no way does it mean they think you're a terrible writer.

Remember that this is business, and editors are buying your work, not praising your abilities. So whilst it may seem like a criticism to have to rewrite your work, it's just part of the profession. You'll often find that editors who've asked for amends are only too happy to commission you again, and the second time around you submit exactly what they're looking for first time.

A word from the editors

"Don't be precious – writing is just the first stage of the process. Expect edits and tweaks. Submit articles that meet the brief: lots of first-time writers don't even bother to read the magazine they're pitching, let alone the guidelines. Read the guidelines, think about what would fit the magazine and write accordingly. When you get a commission keep to the brief and to the word count."

Emily Dubberley, Editor at Large, *Scarlet Magazine*

Tackling rewrites

It's worth noting that when you're writing for newspapers and magazines you will probably never be asked to amend the style of your writing. Rewrite requests pertain almost solely to the content of a piece – expanding this, adding that, or adding the viewpoint of a particular source.

If you are requested to make some changes to an article you've submitted, once again it calls upon your ability to behave as a professional. This means not picking holes or disagreeing with what an editor suggests – even if you think they're being completely unreasonable. When someone comes back to you apparently criticising your hard work, it is a natural response to kick against it and assume they're wrong. But when you've tackled this initial emotional response, you may be forced to concede that the editor has made some valuable points, and some good suggestions for an improved piece. It's certainly easier to make a rewrite when this is the case. But unfortunately, as a freelancer your job is also to add requested changes even if they really are superfluous or strange.

Timescales

Make the amends to the best of your ability, and do it fast. If an editor has a slot picked out for your piece, they often only give themselves a few days to sub and set a piece in their publication, so you should aim to get a rewrite back to them in two days maximum, and preferably on the same day. After all, by this stage your deadline has already passed, so you're effectively submitting a piece on borrowed time. If you really can't get hold of a vital contact or piece of information in that time, phone the editor and explain the situation. Then they can tell you how much time you have for the rewrite.

Incidentally, there is a kind of 'one-off' rule when it comes to editors making excessive demands for rewrites which clearly don't match the original brief. In the interests of professionalism, I would say you should make one rewrite of this type without complaint. You'd be amazed how often an editor who seems like a nightmare on one article suddenly accepts every other piece you do without complaint.

You'll also find that editors almost never request that you rewrite something more than once – it's usually a one-shot deal. They identify what's missing, you change it, they're happy. That's the usual run of things. So you don't need to be too anxious that a piece will keep bouncing back to you like some onerous boomerang.

It wasn't in the brief – unreasonable rewrites

Some editors can however be a little unreasonable in expecting you to put in things in a rewrite which they clearly didn't ask for in the first version. The classic is to ask for box-outs, but editors occasionally come back asking for a different source or a different slant from what was originally suggested.

If you find yourself in the unfortunate circumstance where an editor continually makes requests for material to be rewritten in a clear departure from the original brief or pitch, you're quite within your rights to call them and delicately explain your grievance. Ideally I would recommend calling before you start to write your next piece for them, rather than after a rewrite request. This way you can explain how you're keen to get the brief absolutely solid this time, because you've noticed that the brief and the expectation for the final article haven't quite matched up previously.

This happens very rarely, though. Editors for the most part are very reasonable people who are just as keen as you to have the commissioning process made as smooth as possible.

Learning the hard way: rewrites

I once wrote an article which came back to me no less than four times to be rewritten. It was an article on Paris which I'd written as a lengthy prose piece, but as it turned out (at stark odds with the original brief) needed to be written in short sections on each individual area of the city.

Rather than communicate this request specifically, on my first submission the editor came back asking for 'more facts' to be added, to which I duly obliged. Clearly, this didn't do

---

anything to make the article broken down by area, so he came back and said the facts 'weren't specific enough'. "You state that the Arc De Triumph was built in 1856," he wrote, "but I wanted to know how high it was."

Clearly, the expectation that I could read minds as well as write engaging features was excessive, and I phoned him up and told him so. At which point he admitted that he really wanted a piece more or less identical to one that had run in a rival publication, in which Paris was broken down by area. I also suspect that he had a difficult publisher breathing down his neck telling him the article needed to be a certain way, and the poor man was stuck between a rock and a hard place.

I submitted the piece entirely changed to this new format, and was asked to rewrite it to cover slightly different areas, which I did and the piece finally went to print. Obviously, doing all that extra work in lieu of getting a clear brief in the first place was irksome, but I went on to do quite a few more pieces for the same editor with none of the same problems. We'd both learned from the experience.

Even seasoned professional writers are occasionally asked to make amends to a piece. Writing is a creative process, which means it's open to different interpretations, and because of this the occasional conflict of opinion is bound to arise. For the newcomer, it's simply another chance to show yourself as an excellent writer, by tackling the suggested changes accurately and quickly.

Web tip:
For extra support you can always book in for some training at www.nocontactsnoproblem.com/training.html. You'll often find that other writers can spur you on through the tough times.

Action plan

This is a period to reflect and internalise what you've achieved, and to reaffirm your goal to get into print. If you've already encountered some rejection, remember that this is a necessary part of the process, bringing you nearer to your target. If you're at the stage of supplying a rewrite, remember all the points of professional behaviour listed in this book. Take a moment to write out your reasons for wanting to get into print, and remind yourself to think positive – your goal is nearer than you imagine!

11

Tricks of the trade

Getting into print is one thing, but there are a few tricks of the trade which can make your life as a feature writer much easier. This chapter covers the industry inside knowledge which can help you track down contacts faster, help supply elusive experts for your articles, and get on the journalist guest list for some great events and trips.

In this chapter, you'll:

- Find out how to cut down on your writing time.
- Discover the PR resource.
- Learn about writers' perks and how to get them.
- Know how to galvanise yourself for the long haul.

Congratulations! You've now learned everything you need to know to get into print. It's finally time to go it alone, launching your pitches, chasing up editors and putting in all the necessary work to take your writing to the next level. So in many ways the most exciting part is still to come. Here, we cover a few tricks of the trade to help you turn your work over faster, and get a few expert tips under your belt before you launch your career.

Tricks to get good sources

After you've got started writing full articles, you'll begin to notice that certain factors take up more of your time than others. In particular, the tiresome business of tracking down sources who are able and willing to speak to the press will form a significant part of your workload – not to mention being rather stressful by nature of the uncertainty involved.

When you first start writing, the natural thing is to go to your sources directly. Looking for a lawyer? Ring up a law firm and ask to speak to one. Hoping to speak with an accountant? Run an Internet search and dig up a few email addresses. This strategy makes absolute sense, and can also be a very fast way to get quotes, but once you've been writing a while you'll find it's a method which can also come with a few problems.

What you'll find is for every brilliant garrulous source willing to talk your ear off, you meet with ten rather reticent speakers who sound like they'd really rather you hadn't called. Many people are wary of journalists, and being caught on the spot without time to prepare can make them nervous and paranoid that they'll make some dreadful comment which will go on the record and ruin their lives.

To give you an idea of how intimidating some people find the press, many companies even run media training to allow their staff to practise fielding probing questions from journalists. Ultimately, you might know that you're looking to write a happy article where everyone comes out well, but your source doesn't, so you often have to compensate for their nerves and anxiety.

Adding in a middle-man

You can more or less remove this problem by giving people due warning that you're going to call, and by having someone else in their organisation prime them to confirm that you're a nice person with no agenda to make them look bad. To the uninitiated there are two ways of doing this:

- **Do it yourself.** To a certain extent you can do this yourself by phoning a source directly and explaining to them that you'd like to call back at a convenient time to interview them for ten minutes or so. This is usually enough to reassure people, and gives them the chance to refuse (which they almost never do).

- **Have their organisation do it for you.** The second, and often better, way is to phone through to the press officer, or similarly authorised person, and ask them to set up an interview for you.

Most organisations over a certain size will have their own press department, which will deal with things such as sending out press releases and tackling bad publicity. This, incidentally, is a reason why it can often be easier to approach large companies for quotes rather than SMEs.

In order to make the most of this useful resource, simply phone up and ask to speak to the press department – or if you suspect that the company concerned is not large enough to have this kind of facility, ask to speak to 'whoever deals with media enquiries'. When you're put through, explain who you are and where you're calling from (for the purposes of the enquiry you're an employee of whichever publication you're writing for). Outline your request, and with any luck you'll have magically delegated your quest to find a case study, or relevant expert.

In practice, however, it's often not quite as simple as this. Press departments at many big organisations can be helpful, but for the most part their remit is to defend the organisation against bad press rather than to be instrumental in getting their company coverage. So whilst they may take on the responsibility of finding you someone, it's usually not something they see as central to their job.

Indeed, press departments for academic organisations in particular often tend to see themselves as something of an extra switchboard for this type of enquiry, and will just give you the number of the person you need to contact, so you'll still need to call them cold and explain yourself. Hardly worth your calling through to press in the first place.

Press departments also work to a slower timescale than you might like with this type of enquiry, simply because they have a lot of other things to do. So the usual timescale for a press department to find you someone for a quote is one or two weeks, which – as you'll discover when you've been freelancing for a while – is a very long time.

Last but not least, some (but by no means all) press departments can be quite prickly where journalists are concerned. A key part of their job is to field bad press, after all, so they may see their role as one of defending their company from your kindly attentions, rather than exposing them. This can make them more likely to demand some kind of written agenda or questions from you before they'll consider the request, or worse, even refuse you after keeping you waiting for a week or so for that vital quote.

PRs – your dynamite resource

So what's the solution to these less-than-adequate ways of tracking sources? Although you will still find yourself approaching press departments by necessity in many instances, there is another way to get the information you're after – and at high speed, too. Larger companies in particular hire PRs or Public Relations agencies to get them good coverage and keep their names in the public domain. So when you see a mention of Sainsbury's in a food magazine, for example, it's often because their hard-working PR department has sent a barrage of press releases on such-and-such a product or development to the person who wrote the piece.

Whilst the press department can be cagey about journalists, PRs will be delighted when you get in touch – a big part of their job involves contacting journalists cold and trying to pitch them good stories anyway. They're trying to get their client in the press as much as possible, and this means they will bend over backwards to help you.

How PRs work

To give you a quick inside track on how PRs function, a standard set-up is for them to be held on retainer as long as they get a certain amount of coverage for their client each month. They'll also often have a particular genre or readership count of publications their client needs to be featured in, and for large organisations in particular this can be a very tough target.

A PR representing a famous bank, for example, may have to get several mentions in national newspapers every month, or the bank looks for a new PR. When you start freelancing you'll realise what a high expectation this is. The pressure must be incredible, because PRs essentially only get paid for the toughest bit of your job as a freelancer – pitching and getting a commission, with no fee for a write-up.

The journalist/PR relationship

Journalists are traditionally supposed to be rather disparaging of PRs, as the latter have the disadvantage of being tarred with the 'corporate' brush. So whilst journalists are supposed to be non-partisan, working hard to expose corruption and write only well-researched truths, PRs have the less laudable role of trying to get their clients a mention for profit.

In theory at least, for a journalist to be accepting the help of a PR could jeopardise their impartiality, particularly if the support in question also comes with free lunches or gifts attached. PRs are well known for the age-old 'no such thing as a free lunch' adage, and are employed for their ability to be adept at oiling the wheels of the media machinery for their clients.

In addition, the vast majority of journalists either start off in or work on publications where they are continually approached by PRs anxious for coverage. Sometimes PRs supply great story ideas, but sometimes their ideas are not so good – and some have a bad habit of coming through with a completely irrelevant case study for a story you're writing, just as you're at your busiest.

The moral quandary

The other dilemma for many journalists where PRs are concerned is one of a more practical type. Newspapers and magazines run mainly on the budgets from their advertisers, who pay many thousands of pounds to buy-out page space. If journalists afford a great deal of credence to PRs, thoughtfully plugging their clients and running the stories they suggest, the impetus for an organisation to buy advertising at the publication is greatly diminished. After all, why would the marketing department at a given company spend thousands on ad space, and many thousands more developing advertising to go in the spaces, when for a relatively modest fee a hard-working PR can get them regular coverage – and in the editorial section at that.

To a certain extent then, using news that a PR gives you could undermine the very publication you're working for, by depriving them of their paid adverts later down the line. This might be something you're not overly concerned about. You might be of the opinion that how a newspaper makes its advertising revenue is nothing really to do with you. But it's something you might at least like to bear in mind.

And the advantage

The advantage of PRs is that by their nature, they tend to be highly capable, efficient and personable people – in short, the ideal resource to delegate to. You can rest assured that even if you've forgoten about a particular expert they were handling, they won't; they'll do your job for you, chasing you and arranging suitable interview times.

They'll also often keep in contact after your story has been published, suggesting ideas for you to pitch, sending you press releases, and letting you know when they take on a new client who might be useful to you. PRs can make your job at least 50% easier if you help them to help you.

In addition, issues of corruption really only impact at the higher levels. Most PRs are only too happy to help a hard-working freelancer, but the big budgets tend to be reserved for wooing editors. Whilst you may find the odd lunch, party, or freebie thrown your way, the kind of gifts which could be associated with out-and-out bribery are at the higher end of print media, so you don't really need to worry about compromising your integrity.

The next time you read a national Sunday supplement, however, you might want to ask yourself why such and such a story has run. It could be the result of groundbreaking news. But you might also notice a few features which seem to happily coincide with an all-expenses-paid trip for the editor and their family.

A word from the editors

"Long gone are the days of PRs being seen as 'fluffy' or 'Ab Fab'. Most of the UK media now acknowledges that the relationship between journalists and PRs is co-dependent and each are just as important as the other. PRs can help journalists to develop creative ideas for features and can also put journalists in touch with other professionals and editors in their industry."

Susie Tempest, Director, Saltmarsh PR

Finding the PRs

So where do you find these useful people? Well, to a certain extent, if you're in print, they'll find you. But if you're contacting a large organisation, you can simply ask the reception who handles their

PR, and they will usually give you an outside number. Otherwise, press releases are often written by PRs, who will state themselves as contacts at the bottom along with the title of their company, so you know they're exterior to the one featured in the release.

Web-based alerts and other online resources

In this, the golden age of technology, there is another new and very useful tool for getting hold of good people for quotes – particularly for the first-time writer. The world-wide web has now spawned a handful of journalist alert sites which PRs and other parties interested in press coverage subscribe to.

As a journalist, you need only register your details, type in an alert for whatever contact or information you're after, press send, and hey presto! In minutes your inbox is full of PRs eager to provide you with sources for your article.

This is particularly helpful if you're looking for something which would otherwise be reasonably difficult to track down – say, a person who has retired but gone back to work for their company, or a family who have emigrated to Australia. If you pick the right site then PRs are great for this type of thing, and they will do all the running for you.

There are disadvantages, though. If your request is quite generic, you may find yourself literally flooded with information – to the extent that it's actually quite hard to filter out the useful stuff. And you will also get more than a few responses which simply don't meet the request you've put out, from over-enthusiastic PRs keen to get their clients in the press. This figure goes up the more prestigious the publication you're writing for.

In general, use journalist alert sites if you:

- Need a case study which could be hard to get hold of.
- Are looking for reasonably specific information or statistics.
- Have a very urgent article.
- Need to talk to a specialist or an industry insider with particular knowledge of a niche area.
- Are writing a 'what's new' style piece and are after the latest happenings or product releases.

153

You should probably use your own resources if:

- Your request is very general.
- Many companies are likely to fit the article you're writing.
- The article is likely to cover something quite negative or controversial.

You can find a list of good journalist alert sites in the Useful Information section at the back of this book, or at www.nocontacts noproblem.com/links.

And how would you like to receive alerts from real-life editors, desperate to find a freelancer to cover a particular topic? Believe it or not, this does happen, despite the competitiveness of the industry (and the fact that in theory at least, editors should have dozens of writers 'on file').

It doesn't happen very often, but when it does, these requests usually take the form of an online alert – identical to the alerts which you'll be sending for information, but this time it's an editor requesting writers.

With this in mind, there are some good sites to subscribe to updates and some potentially good ideas. You can find a list of recommended sites in the Useful Information section at the back of this book, or at www.nocontactsnoproblem.com/links.

Writers' perks

I'm going to let you into a little secret. You know all those great perks you hear about journalists getting? Free trips abroad, great parties and all manner of lovely freebies? It's not just staff journalists who get them. Freelancers get these perks too, and what's more, we sometimes get them even better.

Learning the hard way: freelance perks

When I was starting out, I did some work experience for the Sunday Telegraph Magazine, *who, as you might imagine, were privy to plenty of freebies. Every week the food editor compiled a page of the latest food products, all of which would arrive in the offices for photographing. The same would happen for the interiors pages, the gardening section, the beauty editor's desk and so on. The companies who sent these products weren't expecting them back. For the most part they averaged less than £20 in price, and were worth an absolute fortune in free advertising to the manufacturers when recommended on the pages of a national magazine.*

At the end of the week, all of these lovely artefacts were put on a big table, and everyone got their pick. That was the theory. But in reality the process was subject to something of a hierarchy in terms of who got what. In addition everything was divided out amongst all of the staff, and no one wanted to appear greedy with what they were making off with.

As a freelancer, however, anything you get sent is yours, all yours. So if you were to write an article on vodka and had samples of every bottle you were writing about sent to you for tasting, you'd be free to keep the lot without dividing it out between everyone in the office.

The type of freebies which companies send out to get themselves in the press are by no means limited to staff writers. In fact, companies often prefer freelancers, because in theory (and often in practice) they can get them represented in several different publications, whereas a staff writer can only plug them in one.

The catch is that you don't have items sent with anywhere near the same frequency of well-known publications. When I worked on a food magazine we had hampers of food items couriered in several times a day on the off-chance that we might write about them. As a freelancer this almost never happens. But you are quite within your rights to phone up PRs and ask for particular products to be sent if they suit an article you're writing.

There are limits on this. If you go above a certain amount in value, or you're requesting a particularly unusual item, you may need to send it back in perfect condition. Fashion is one area where everything has to go back, whilst in areas like technology, items above the £60 mark will be expected to be returned. But everything else you request and write about is fair game, and you won't have to share it with other staff or justify under the beady eye of an editor why your desk is filling up with free products.

If you write about travel or food you can also get certain services for free, such as a night or two in a hotel, a restaurant meal, or a few cocktails in a bar. This is on the understanding that you will be reviewing the establishment, and obviously you need to honour this in print.

How do you get the freebies?

You ask. Speak to whichever company has the product or establishment you want to review. Talk to someone at the press department, and see if they are able to help you. It goes without saying that you should always represent any product or service you receive fairly in whichever publication you've promised, but you'll be surprised how often the chance to get your hands on free items comes up. Even someone working on an employment piece, for example, could review the latest office technologies.

For other perks like press trips and parties, you have to be known to PR agencies who will have a list of people to invite. If you're a name on a list of potential journalists in a certain field, you could find yourself in the running for a number of appealing perks.

Parties

When it comes to parties, you can quite easily get yourself a slew of invites, because PRs generally like to have journalists at their events in any capacity. If you think about it, if you were a company launching some product or other and your PR company threw you a party at which you constantly bumped into journalists, you'd be quite impressed by their clout.

If you're invited to a party by a PR, you're really not necessarily expected to write about whatever it is they're profiling at the event, because it's sort of a symbiotic arrangement. You show up, add a bit of prestige by merit of being a journalist, and they give you a few free drinks and canapés. Obviously they'd like you to bear their client or product in mind, and you're certainly more likely to find yourself on ever-better party lists if you manage to feature a PR's client shortly after being introduced to them at a party.

Press trips

Of course the real bonus of getting onto PR lists is that you may find yourself invited on a press trip. These can be in a number of capacities outside travel, as PRs know that offering free travel is a great way to get journalists to attend an event. So whilst the majority of trips will be for travel writers, there are plenty of trips for food writers, for example, to experience the manufacturing process of products in their native lands, or property writers to find out about new projects abroad.

Last-minute invites

As a freelancer you often find yourself in the dubious category of being a back-up guest. Staff journalists can be incredibly blasé about a PR's time when they're organising events, and you'd be shocked at how many bow-out at the last minute.

You'd also be amazed by how often staff journalists are forced to turn down trips of a lifetime because their editors are too mean to let them go. It seems perfectly obvious to me that there are few better motivators to get your work done on time than the promise of a great trip away, but editors don't always see it that way. More importantly, it often falls to the hierarchy that editors magically find the time to go on all the best trips, leaving little to be shared out amongst the rest of the staff. But even editors are under pressure to at least appear that they're in the office a reasonable amount. As a freelancer, if you really want to go on a trip you can make the time, which gives you an enormous advantage over staffers.

Learning the hard way: getting on press trips
If you talk with a PR, they've often been forced to contact literally hundreds of editors about a particular trip or occasion, because a lot refuse and others accept and then change their minds. Personally, I think this is tremendously rude – after all, I doubt many journalists would suddenly change their minds about a holiday they'd organised and paid for with their own money.

The upside of this situation is that if you prove yourself reliable, polite and personable you'll be one step above a lot of editors, who sometimes think they have a right to be rude to PRs. I even worked with one editor who phoned up a PR to complain because a free bottle of wine she'd been sent had broken her corkscrew!

Be well-mannered at all times, reply faithfully to invites and attend every event you are asked to, and you'll probably put yourself top of a PR's list for a last-minute trip.

It might be irksome for a PR, but as a freelancer, drop-outs are great news, because you may find yourself contacted at the eleventh hour by a PR with space on a trip which they're desperate to fill. It doesn't look good if a PR is unable to find enough journalists to send away on their client's money, so as a rule they'd prefer a journalist who perhaps didn't have a firm commission but might sell the piece later than no journalist at all.

Obviously, if you are lucky enough to be offered one of these last-minute places, you'll have to decide whether you think you can get it coverage, as this really is an unspoken (or sometimes highly vocalised) part of the deal.

Make the most of perks – they're part of your pay

As you can see, there are a lot of perks available to freelancers, particularly if you're writing regularly for top publications, and I recommend that you fully enjoy them. The publishing world incidentally has a bad habit of creating a sort of myth that perks are nothing to do with journalism, and a low salary and long hours are reward enough.

I would argue that with staff pay and conditions almost always being poor, perks should form a valuable part of your final pay packet. After all, journalism is supposed to be a glamorous profession, so you'd be doing your career a disservice not to balance the monetary rewards with the extras which come for free. This can also allow you to save a little money in the course of your professional life, which when you're starting out is no bad thing.

Web tip:
For a comprehensive list of 'tricks of the trade' websites, from PR request sites to industry updates, you can go to
www.nocontactsnoproblem.com/resources.html

12

And finally...

Marketing is all

You're now at the end of your 'No Contacts' training, and are hopefully well set up to go it alone. But before sending you on your way to enjoy a successful life in print, it's important that we reiterate the most important insider tactic of all.

Perks, parties and press trips are one thing, but your most important trick of the trade as a freelancer is that you are your own hard-working marketing machine. This is vital to retaining your motivation, and, crucially – *to not taking rejection personally.* You may be talented, full of great ideas, and the best writer in the world, but I guarantee you that what will count more towards your success is an inexhaustible stock of professional determination.

Make no mistake that your efforts and ideas will be knocked back – often – and it will be difficult. But when you're dealing with the inevitable rejection which comes with being freelance, always remember this:

REMEMBER: **It's not your writing, it's the way you're marketing it.**

Sadly there are all too many great journalists and even better writers out there who give up or stay low on funds, not because they don't have the talent to do the job, but because they are not selling it effectively. Vincent Van Gogh didn't die an impoverished artist because he couldn't paint. He failed to realise the income he deserved during his lifetime because his work wasn't marketed correctly. And whilst you might argue that this technique produced some very fine creations, I doubt you'd prefer to be remembered for your genius posthumously than to be paid a proper salary in vivo.

Writing is a highly subjective craft, and during the course of your career it is more likely than not that you will come across someone who doesn't like your writing style. You need to be able to weigh these opinions against the many people who will like (and buy) your work, and not let the negative views interfere with your ability to sell it with confidence. So have faith in yourself always and at all times – you can and will get your work in print.

And when you do, perhaps you'd like to give others some tips on your success on our 'No Contacts' forum:
www.nocontactsnoproblem/forum.html

The entrepreneurial curve

The other thing I want you to be aware of when you're starting out is that you're at the toughest stage, and the toughest stage lasts longer than you think. Before you get to the stage of regular work and the odd nice perk thrown your way, you're probably going to experience something called the 'entrepreneurial curve.'

With every business starting out there is a correlation between the effort which goes in and the rewards paid out – but this might not necessarily follow the trajectory you expect. For most logical people, if they put in 'x' they get out 'y', and this relationship would follow a line which looks something like this:

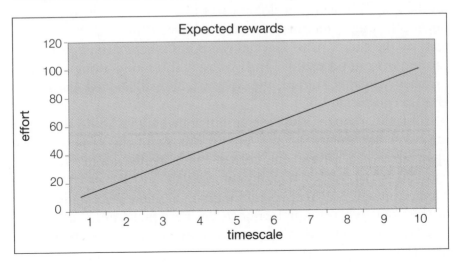

But here's the problem. All of the research which has gone into start-up businesses shows that the reality of their growth is not a straight line, but a curve – something more like this:

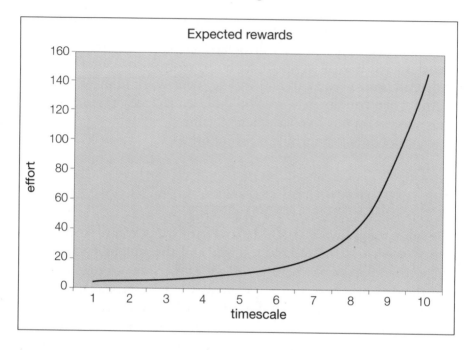

As you can see from the second picture, the rewards actually come much thicker and faster than you might expect once you've ridden out the initial slower rise. When you're in the lower point on the graph, however, it doesn't feel like this – it feels like you're putting in huge amounts of effort with very limited rewards. In fact, by the time you've reached the point where you expect to be turning over good profits, and you're still limping along similarly to when you first started, you might feel disillusioned enough to give up completely.

Ironically, though, most entrepreneurs who give up do so just as the curve has started to pick up. At this point the rather sudden upsweep is just around the corner, but it really doesn't feel that way. So when you're starting out freelancing, be aware of this curve. You will probably spend longer than you expect building up to the point where your freelance business picks up. But – **don't give up**. Your rewards will come eventually, and they will more than repay your efforts.

A word from the editors

"In competitive industries like media, it's really all about persistence. A lot of people in TV or journalism will talk about how they had some lucky break or other, but when you question them more closely you find that they worked hard for a long time to be in the position to get that break, and kept going through countless near misses. My advice for getting into the writing business comes from the strap-line of Galaxy Quest – 'never give up, never surrender!'."

Neil Richards, Screen Writer

Action plan

You're now ready to move onto the four-week plan to kick-start your writing career. Remember the advice so far, and focus on garnering your faith in your writing ability for the journey ahead.

13

The four-week plan

Ready to kick start your freelance career? If you're able to put aside a few hours a day for four weeks, you can give yourself the best possible chance of getting into print fast by following this four-week plan.

You will need some of that time to be during the daytime so you can make phone calls to chase up editors, but generally speaking the actions laid out should be able to fit in with the average nine-to-five job. Just so long as you can grab a half-hour on your lunch break here and there.

Overview of the plan

The next four weeks will look something like this:

1   Week One – building a list to pitch.

2   Week Two – pitching and writing clips.

3   Week Three – pitching and writing clips.

4   Week Four – chasing, writing clips, and finding clip outlets.

You should try and follow the plan as consecutive weeks, but there is some leeway if you were forced to take a week out and move the tasks for the next week forwards. Try to pick a month when you know you should have some free time, and make a proper commitment to the cause – you may have to sacrifice some social occasions to get into print.

Week one

Already built a list to pitch? This week that list is going to become much, much bigger. Rather than trying out a few pitches with likely editors, you're now building the foundations of your entire freelance practice. So this week is about getting those names and publications down which will form the stalwart of your pitching strategy.

Day One	Find twenty publications of likely interest using the tips laid out in Chapters 1 and 2.
Day Two	Find ten publications of likely interest and contact five editors using the tips in Chapter 2.
Day Three	Find ten publications of likely interest and contact five editors.
Day Four	Contact ten editors.
Day Five	Contact ten editors.

By the end of the week you should have at least ten editors ready and willing to look at your pitches.

Week two

Ready to get your imagination into gear? This week you'll be working on a combination of pitching and writing yourself some clips to use as evidence of your work.

Day One	Choose an editor who will receive three pitches from you by the end of the week. Write one pitch for them and decide on a subject for a clip example of your work which you will write this week. It should be on a subject of relevance to the editors you are pitching.
Day Two	Spend an hour writing your clip – remember you can use fictional quotes in this piece – and an hour writing up your second pitch for the editor you've chosen.
Day Three	Follow the same structure as yesterday, with an hour writing your clip and an hour writing the third and final pitch.
Day Four	Send your pitches out to the relevant editor, and spend an hour reworking them to be of relevance to a further two editors who cover the same subject. Send them out. Now take an hour to continue writing your clip.
Day Five	Rework the pitches you have and send them to another two editors. Spend an hour writing your clip.

By the end of this week you should have pitched five different editors and finished writing an article for print. If you still have a bit of work to do on your article and pitches, make sure it's completed by the end of the week. Proof-read the article and have it checked for sense and flow. Don't be tempted to send it off, though – no matter how good it is. Only pitches should be sent as examples of your work.

Week three

This week you're continuing to build on the foundations you laid last week, pitching to editors and building clips for yourself.

Day One	Choose an editor who will receive three pitches from you by the end of the week. Write one pitch for them and decide on a subject for a clip example of your work which you will write this week. It should be on a subject of relevance to the editors you are pitching.
Day Two	Spend an hour writing your clip – remember you can use fictional quotes in this piece – and an hour writing up your second pitch for the editor you've chosen.
Day Three	Follow the same structure as yesterday, with an hour writing your clip and an hour writing the third and final pitch.
Day Four	Send your pitches out to the relevant editor, and spend an hour reworking them to be of relevance to a further two editors who cover the same subject. Send them out. Now take an hour to continue writing your clip.
Day Five	Rework the pitches you have and send them to another two editors. Spend an hour writing your clip.

By the end of this week you should have pitched five different editors and finished writing an article for print. If you still have a bit of work left to do on your article and pitches, make sure it's completed by the end of the week. Proof-read the article and have it checked for sense and flow.

Week four

This week you've left enough time to check back with the editors you pitched in Week Two. But be aware that you haven't left much time to assess your pitches, so this is more of a call to see that they've arrived safely and are being considered. You'll have only five editors this week who qualify for a chase-up, so spend a few minutes every day tracking them down and asking after your work.

Day One	Chase editors. Choose and start writing your third clip. Spend an hour looking for potential outlets for clips as discussed in Chapter 6.
Day Two	Chase editors. Continue writing your third clip. Spend an hour looking for potential outlets for clips.
Day Three	Chase editors. Continue writing your third clip. Spend an hour looking for potential outlets for clips.
Day Four	Chase editors. Continue writing your third clip. Spend an hour looking for potential outlets for clips
Day Five	Chase editors. Continue writing your third clip. Spend an hour looking for potential outlets for clips.

By the end of this week you should have made contact with all five editors you pitched in Week Two, and come back with some good responses. In reality it's quite likely that one or two editors may have been completely uncontactable for some reason. In this case, simply send a chase-up email and make sure you log them properly by whatever method you're using to keep track of your pitches (see Chapter 5).

If you've followed the plan conscientiously, you should now have:

- Pitched ten editors three ideas each.
- Written three good clips which you can send as evidence of your work.
- Tracked down some good potential outlets to publish your work unpaid for the purposes of building a clip library, and secured a space for at least one article to get into print.
- Chased up five editors.

You should be very proud of what you've achieved this month – it's a heavy workload if you're working full-time, but rest assured that you've made vital progress towards getting yourself into print. By now you should have a good idea of how to continue. You'll chase up those extra five editors who've been sent your ideas, find some new ones to pitch, and get some more of your ideas out there. But now you've got the machinery truly up and running, the process should come far more easily than you've imagined.

Good luck, and remember to share tips with other writers and keep us posted on your progress on the 'No Contacts' forum: www.nocontactsnoproblem.com/forum.html

Useful information and further reading

As I mentioned in the introduction to this book, there are plenty of good resources out there to help you branch out in your writing career once you've got started. Here are some that I recommend.

Books

The Freelance Writer's Handbook by Andrew Croft
The Well-Fed Writer by Robert Bly
What Color is Your Parachute by Richard Bolles
Ready, Aim, Specialize! by Kelly James-Enger

All of these books are available via
www.nocontactsnoproblem.com/books.html

Journalist alert sites

Response Source – www.responsesource.com
Well-established, dedicated journalist alert site with many PR subscribers delivering very good results.

Getting Ink – www.gettingink.typepad.com
This alert system is part of a wider writers' forum, which means you can also get help from fellow journalists, and the site is severe on PRs who respond with irrelevant material. Currently less well subscribed than Response Source, but good for covering all bases.

ProfNet – www. profnet.prnewswire.com

This site differentiates itself by being aimed mainly at experts and professionals like university lecturers and other specialists. The nature of the audience means that responses are usually less 'can do' than those from PRs, but it can be a helpful way to get hold of a willing expert if you fear that your request may overload you with responses from other sites.

Sourcewire – www.sourcewire.com

The original birthplace of Response Source, this site deals specifically with technology requests and is very useful if you have a query relating to this subject.

Food4Media – www.food4media.com

This site requires you to register, but once you have, as the name suggests, it is a good site for food-based enquiries. This can include tracking down case studies from the hospitality industry, or bar and hotel requests. PR subscribers tend to be more geared to the consumer press, so if your article is for a trade, response might be less effusive, but generally a good choice for food queries. You can also upload your own photo and biography for editors to search you out, and recive alerts about new writing opportunities.

TravMedia – www.travmedia.com

From the same people as Food4Media, but generally more open to trades as well as consumer titles. This is an excellent site for travel requests, particularly if you're looking for 'what's new' type information and good quality images. As with Food4Media you can also upload your own profile and receive job alerts.

Other online resources

Get yourself on the mailing list for these sites to receive media alerts and even the occasional urgent request for writers.

www.gorkana.com

www.news4media.com – an umbrella site for a comprehensive gamut of alert sites covering everything from health to fashion to technology to property.

Index

advertising strategies 41
articles, writing 123–124
   content 127–130
   length of time to write
      125–126
   using quotes 130

box-outs 114
brainstorming 54
briefs, types of 110–111

chase-ups 91–106
   how to chase-up 94–97
      by phone 95–96
      by email 95
   importance of 94
clips 70–90
   celebrity interviews 81–84
   C–list celebrities 82
   getting 71–72, 79
   Word documents 75
commissions
   getting 3
      by email 108
      by phone 108–109
   first commissions 107–108
confidence 48
copyright 116–117

deadlines 112–113
dpi 133

editors, contacting 31–36
   initial phone call 32–34
   key questions 35–36
entrepreneurial curve 161–162
expendex 120–121

fees, negotiating 139–141
first serial rights 117–118
four-week plan 164–169
full-time writing 137–138

giffs 134
groundwork 8

headline 44, 58
head-sell 5, 41, 44, 59

ideas
   finding an angle 57–58
   keymarkets for 26
   unidentified trends 53
interviewing 131

Jasc Paint 133
Jpeg 134

literary style 39

marketing 160–161
markets
  for freelancers 14–21
    consumer magazines
      16–17
    consumer newspapers
      14–15
    local papers 20
    national newspapers 15,
      27
    trade magazines 18–19
    trade publications 14
    online publications
      20–21
  researching 10–12

NUJ rates of payment 139

'on-spec' writing 114–115
online resources 153

pay, rates of 112
Photoshop 133
pictures 119–120
  size of 133
pitches
  fitting your pitch to the
    market 40–41
  keeping track of 101–102
    databases 103–105
      advanced 104–105
      basic 103–104
  structuring
    bulleted list 60–61
    headed list 62–63
    head-sell 59–60
    letter 61–62

written list 103
how to send
  hard copy 66–67
  email 67–68
using experts 45
writing a good pitch 4
pitching
  by networking 87
  by phone 86
  elements to a winning
    pitch 39–40
  face-to-face 86–87
  formats 58–59
  grammar and layout
    43–44
  ideas 2, 39, 45, 46, 52
  random 9
  style of 46
  to the right person 68
press departments 149
professionalism 47–48
PRs 150–153
publication formats 28–29

rejection 12, 98–100, 137, 160
research 38, 42
rewrites 141–144
  tackling 143
  timescales 143
  unreasonable rewrites
    144–145

self-esteem 11, 49
specialist markets 24–25, 29
  subjects
    to avoid
    recommended subject
      areas 25–26
standfirst 5, 28, 44, 58

student publications 79
supporting material 54–55
synopsis 4
tiffs 134

websites 85

word count 111–112
work experience 2, 77, 88
writer's perks 154–157
    parties 156–157
    press trips 157